Protein-Balanced Vegetarian Cookery

David Scott

Illustrations by
Steve Hardstaff

CRCS PUBLICATIONS
Post Office Box 1460
Sebastopol, California 95472

Library of Congress Cataloging-in-Publication Data

Scott, David, 1944–
  Protein-balanced vegetarian cookery.

  Bibliography: p.
  Includes index.
  1. Vegetarian cookery. I. Title.
TX837.S33 1988   641.5'636   87–3459
ISBN 0-916360-39-3

FIRST U.S.A. EDITION—Originally published in Great Britain
by Rider Books, Century Hutchinson Ltd.

INTERNATIONAL STANDARD BOOK NUMBER: 0-916369-39-3

Published in the United States by CRCS Publications

Distributed in the United States by
CRCS Publications

Contents

...NOTE FOR AMERICAN EDITION: The American equivalents to English terms and measurements can be found on pages 172 & 174.

Acknowledgements

I would particularly like to thank Sally Robertson, fine cook and restaurant manageress, for supplying thirty-five of the recipes used in this book. My thanks also to Rita Trotter who typed the manuscript so expertly that finding a typing error became a challenge.

Introduction

The intention of this book is to offer a straightforward guide to how, and why, we can enjoy a healthy, balanced and high-quality protein diet without eating meat or fish. As well as protein, the body needs a balance of carbohydrates, vitamins and minerals; these needs have also been considered in the recipes chosen for this book.

The main sources of protein in a lacto-vegetarian* diet are grains, pulses, milk, milk products, eggs, nuts and seeds. Eaten in the right quantity and combination these foods can provide protein of a very high quality, enough even for the needs of an energetic sports person, manual worker or growing child. Whole grains, pulses and vegetables also supply carbohydrates and proteins in correct complex proportions for good stamina; many athletes, including the author, taking part in endurance events such as marathon running, have discovered that a diet based on these foods suits them well.

The book is divided into four main sections. The first gives nutritional information and explains what proteins are, how the body uses them, what foods contain them and how particular foods complement one another in protein supply. The second section gives basic recipes for preparing and cooking all the common grains, pulses and nuts. The third section provides a selection of exciting, unusual and tasty high-protein recipes which, when eaten alone or with the recommended supplementary dishes, will supply at least two-fifths, and usually more, of the average adult daily protein requirement. (Note however, that nutritional requirements not only differ from person to person but also vary with time and circumstances.) There are also recipes for breads, salads, spreads, sauces and desserts to accompany and/or supplement the nutrient content of the high protein meals. The final section gives a useful culinary, botanical and nutritional introduction to the commonly available pulses and nuts,

* Throughout the book, when I say 'vegetarian' I mean a lacto-vegetarian, that is, someone who includes milk, milk products and eggs in their diet. I do not mean a vegan, who relies solely on plant food for all nutritional needs.

and line drawings illustrate each one. I hope this latter part of the book and the section on basic cookery methods will be particularly helpful to anyone who is bewildered by the wide variety of grains, pulses and nuts now available in wholefood and health stores and good supermarkets.

The nutritional information and recipes given in the book are accurate but the reader should be aware that nutrition is a complicated and sometimes controversial subject. In the last analysis, finding the right diet for your own needs depends on your own awareness of how the foods you eat affect you. The best diet is naturally the one that makes you feel good, alert, and glad to be you.

Part One:
Nutrition

The balanced diet

For growth, maintenance, energy, repair and regulation of metabolic processes the body needs proteins, carbohydrates, fats, vitamins and minerals. For a healthy and energy-giving diet, all five groups are needed in the right balance. Proteins are needed for growth, repair and maintenance of bodily tissues. Carbohydrates and fats provide energy for the body's activities and fats are also the source of the fat-soluble vitamins A, D, E and K. Vitamins and minerals are required in very small amounts but they are essential to the efficient functioning and regulation of all the body's processes.

Proteins

The proteins the body needs are composed of twenty-two amino acids. Eight of these acids, called the essential amino acids (EAA) cannot be synthesized by the body and must be supplied in the food we eat. All eight EAA are required simultaneously and each must be in the correct proportion to the others if the body is to use them efficiently. Fortunately for us, food proteins normally contain all eight EAA, although one or more may be present in a disproportionately small amount. This small amount of one amino acid limits the usable amount of the remaining essential amino acids, since the body must be provided with them all at the same time in exactly the correct profile. The EAA in short supply is called the limiting EAA and it affects the biological value (the percentage of protein present that can be utilized) of a particular foodstuff. Fortunately the amino acid in short supply in one food is often available in excess in another and vice-versa. By combining two or more complementary foods in one meal we obtain protein of much higher quality or biological value than the total obtained from eating the foods separately. For instance, most grains (e.g. rice, wheat, corn) or grain products are high in the amino acid tryptophan but low in lysine while most pulses (e.g. beans, peas, lentils) are high in lysine and low in tryptophan. Thus a dish containing, say, rice and lentils would supply protein of higher biological value than the same total weight of just rice or just lentils.

The main sources of protein for vegetarians, as may be seen from the table below, are grains, pulses, milk, milk products (e.g. cheese and yoghurt), eggs, nuts and seeds.

The combinations of vegetarian food groups that advantageously complement their individual biological values are:

1. Milk, cheese, yoghurt or other milk products either in or with any dish containing grains, pulses, nuts or seeds.
2. Grains either whole or as a flour product either in or with any dish containing pulses or dairy products.
3. Pulses either in or with any dish containing grains, dairy products or nuts and seeds.

The high protein recipes given in this book were selected on the basis of these complementary protein combinations. Very approximately, the average amount of usable protein in a diet based on a combination of grains, pulses, dairy products, nuts and seeds is 70 to 75 per cent of total protein intake. This is the same figure as for the average meat-orientated diet but without the attendant problem of a high intake of saturated fats.

Table 1   *Biological Value of Particular Foodstuffs* ★

Food group	Biological value (Percentage of protein usable by the body)
Ideal Protein	100
Whole egg	95
Milk	80–85
Cheese	70–75
Mixed diet of whole grains, pulses, dairy products, nuts and seeds	70–75
Meat (muscle)	70–75
Brown rice	70–75
Whole wheat	65–70
Maize (corn)	50–60
Wheat flour (white)	50
Pulses	40–60
Nuts and seeds	35–55

★ Remember these figures only consider protein content. They do not take into account fat, fibre, vitamin, mineral or carbohydrate content.

To compare the biological values of the different food groups eaten on their own or in combination see Table 1. For average daily protein requirements for children and adults see Table 2. For the protein contents of popular lacto-vegetarian foodstuffs, including those used in the recipes given in this book, see Table 3.

Table 2 *Average Daily Requirements of Protein**

	Average height inches (cm)		Average weight pounds (kg)		Protein† (grams)
Infants from birth to 1 year					20
Infants from 1 year to 3 years					23
Children 4 to 6 years	44	(112)	44	(20)	30
Children 7 to 10 years	52	(132)	62	(28)	34
Children 11 to 14 years	62	(157)	99	(45)	45
Teenager (male) 15 to 18 years	69	(176)	145	(66)	56
Teenager (female) 15 to 18 years	64	(163)	120	(55)	46
Adult male	70	(177)	154	(70)	56
Adult female	64	(163)	120	(55)	46

* Extracted from a table of recommended daily dietary allowances published by Food and Nutrition Board, National Academy of Sciences – USA. Revised 1980. Designed for the maintenance of good nutrition of practically all healthy people in the USA.

† Remember protein requirements differ considerably between individuals and even two people the same age, weight, sex and occupation may have very different needs. Figures given here are averages designed to take in a broad range of requirements.

Table 3 *Protein and Calorie Content of Popular Lacto-Vegetarian Protein Foods (all figures per 100 grams edible portion)*

	Protein (grams)	Calories
Dairy produce		
Fresh milk (whole)	3·4	65
(skimmed)	3·5	35
Hen's egg (whole)	12·5	147
Yoghurt (low fat)	5·0	52
Cheddar cheese (and similar e.g. Cheshire, Gruyère)	25	406

Table 3 (continued)

	Protein (grams)	Calories
Soft French cheese (e.g. Camembert, Brie)	23	300
Parmesan	35	400
Edam	24	400
Cottage cheese	13·6	95
Cream cheese	3·1	439
Grains (raw)		
Barley (pot)	9·6	348
Buckwheat	11·7	335
Bulgar wheat	11·2	354
Cornmeal (whole)	9·2	355
Millet	9·9	327
Oatmeal (rolled oats)	14·2	390
Rice (brown)	7·5	360
(white)	6·7	361
Rye (wholemeal)	12·1	334
Sorghum	11·0	332
Wheat flour		
(100% wholemeal)	13·2	318
(85% brown)	12·8	327
(72% white)	9·8	350
Nuts and seeds		
Almonds	18·6	598
Brazils	14·3	654
Cashews	17·2	561
Chestnuts (fresh)	2·9	194
(dried)	6·7	377
Hazelnuts	12·6	620
Pine nuts	31·1	552
Pistachios	19·3	594
Pumpkin seeds	29.0	553
Sesame seeds	18·6	563
Sunflower seeds	24·0	560
Walnuts (black)	20·5	628

Pulses (raw)

Aduki beans	25·3	325
Black-eyed beans	22·8	340
Broad beans	25·1	338
Chickpeas	20·5	360
Haricot beans	21·4	340
Kidney beans (red)	22·4	343
Lentils	24·0	340
Mung beans	24·2	340
Peas	21·1	340
Peanuts (fresh with skins)	24·3	570
Soya (beans)	34·1	403
(beancurd)	8·8	72
(miso)	10·5	171

Carbohydrates

Carbohydrates are the body's main source of energy. They are present in foods as starches and sugars. Starch is obtained from cereal grains and their products, pulses, vegetables, especially root vegetables, and nuts. The complex combination of starches and protein in these foods is a good one for people involved in manual work or sport. Naturally occurring sugars are found in fruits, honey and milk. Refined sugar, added liberally to so many foods, should be used moderately. It lacks every nutrient except carbohydrate and it tends, by spoiling the appetite, to displace from the diet other foods containing the nutrients we need.

Fats

Fats provide a concentrated energy source and the essential fat-soluble vitamins A, D and E. Every fat or oil contains active (unsaturated) or inactive (saturated) acids or both. The active acids are called essential fatty acids (EFA). They are contained in the polyunsaturated fats recommended by many authorities over saturated fats with the aim of helping to prevent heart disease. The saturated fats we eat come generally from animal sources such as meat, butter, cream or cheese. In the recipes in this book, vegetable oils (sunflower, olive, safflower and sesame seed oils are the best), polyunsaturated margarines and low fat cheeses or other milk products are recommended when possible. The author suggests that fats of any description, particularly saturated fats, are used in only moderate amounts. A considerable body of specialists are now of the opinion that the risk of heart disease, high blood pressure and some cancers can be reduced by cutting saturated fat intake. Incidentally, lacto-vegetarians probably have a higher intake of saturated fats (because of milk products in their diets) than vegans but a lower one than meat eaters.

See Table 4 for the unsaturated and saturated fat contents of common oils and fats.

Table 4   *Unsaturated and Saturated Fat Contents of Oils, Fats and Dairy Produce*

Fat/oil	Fat content (percentage of total)	Polyunsaturated fat content	Monosaturated fat content	Saturated fat content
Butter	81	2	34	57
Margarine (average unsaturated)	81	36	38	23
Margarine (average saturated)	81	17	58	22
Corn oil	100	53	28	10
Olive oil	100	7	76	11
Peanut oil	100	29	47	18
Safflower oil	100	72	15	8
Sesame oil	100	42	38	14
Sunflower oil	100	63	19	13
Walnut oil	100	66	15	11
Dairy Product				
Camembert	26	3	29	63
Cheddar	33	3	30	62
Cottage	4	3	27	65
Edam	28	2	28	65
Feta	25	3	22	70
Gouda	27	2	28	64
Gruyère	32	5	31	58
Mozzarella	19	3	30	61
Parmesan	26	2	29	63
Ricotta	15	3	28	64
Milk (whole)	3·5	4	29	63
(skimmed)	2	4	29	60
Yoghurt (whole)	3·4	3	27	65
(low fat)	1·5	3	27	67

Vitamins and minerals

The body cannot synthesize the vitamins and minerals it requires and they must be supplied in the food we eat. The vitamins and minerals are an unrelated group of substances but their functions in the body are interrelated and they are all required in the right balance. A mixed diet of whole grains, pulses, dairy products, vegetables, including salads and fresh fruits, will normally provide all the vitamins and minerals we need.

Fibre

Fibre is found in unrefined cereals, fruit and vegetables. It is not a nutrient because it is not digested, but because it adds bulk to the body's waste products it is essential to efficient elimination.

General rules for a healthy diet

A varied diet of natural foods composed mainly of whole grains or whole grain products, fresh vegetables and fruits, dried (not tinned) pulses, unhydrogenated vegetable oils, nuts, seeds and dairy products in moderation, will supply all the nutrients you need. Natural foods taste better than refined foods and their nutrient and fibre content is always higher. A diet composed mainly of refined foods, often full of sugar and additives, saturated fats and too much salt, is definitely bad for your health. However, having said that, it does no harm to eat a slice of white bread or have more cream than you really need just occasionally. Moderation and self-awareness of your own needs are the touchstones of a good diet and an obsession with proper eating, like an obsession with overeating, causes tension and bad digestion.

As a general guide, the main meal of the day should provide approximately 50 per cent of the protein you need, one light meal should provide about 25 per cent and breakfast about 25 per cent. Each meal should contain two or more major protein sources and at least one meal should include two or more lightly cooked fresh vegetables and a fresh salad (including a leafy green vegetable). Fresh fruit (including citrus fruits), three or four times a day, completes the day's requirements.

Main Lacto-Vegetarian Protein Sources

Grains

Barley (whole)
Buckwheat and buckwheat
  flour
Corn and cornmeal
Millet
Rice (brown)
Rolled oats and oatmeal
Rye and rye flour
Wholewheat, wholemeal flour,
  bulgar (cracked wheat), cous-
  cous, wheat germ and bran

Pulses

Aduki beans
Black-eyed beans
Chickpeas (garbanzos)
Kidney beans (including red
  beans and haricot beans)
Lentils
Peas
Soya beans, soya flour, tofu and
  miso

Cheeses (low to medium fat)

Cheddar
Cottage cheese

Emmenthal
Gouda
Gruyère
Mozzarella
Parmesan
Ricotta

Nuts

Almonds
Brazils
Cashews
Hazels
Peanuts (classified as a pulse)
Pine nuts (pignolias)
Walnuts

Seeds

Sesame
Sunflower

Dairy products

Eggs
Milk (liquid skimmed milk
  preferably)
Yoghurt (low fat, natural
  flavours)

Part Two:
Basic Methods of Preparation

Grains

Cereal grains, either whole or as unrefined flour, are an excellent, well-balanced source of protein and other nutrients. The recipes given here provide basic methods for cooking the whole or milled common grains so that they may be eaten either on their own, as an accompaniment to a meal, or in simple combinations with other ingredients. For more elaborate grain dishes, see the high-protein recipes.

Wheat

Wholewheat

Cooked wholewheat grains (sometimes called berries) make surprisingly tasty and satisfying dishes, and eating the whole grain ensures you get all the nutritious goodness of the wheat. Wholewheat can also be used to make excellent salads if mixed with salad vegetables and dressing or with cooked beans. The latter mixture is an especially rich protein combination.

The grains are prepared for cooking by soaking in water for 3 to 4 hours. They are then cooked in the same way as brown rice. Wholewheat is far more fibrous than rice, however, and never cooks to the same softness. For this reason it is much harder to overcook wholewheat than rice. In most dishes where you would use brown rice, wholewheat can be substituted.

Plain Boiled Wholewheat   *Serves 4*

2 pt (1·1 litres) water
1 lb (450 g) wholewheat berries,
   soaked and drained
1 teaspoon salt

Bring the water to a rolling boil. Add the wheat to the boiling water, return mixture to the boil, reduce heat and simmer for 1½ hours or until the wheat is cooked to the softness you require. Add salt towards the end of cooking time.

To speed up the cooking time, dry roast the wheat in a hot frying pan for 2 to 3 minutes before adding it to the boiling water.

Wholewheat and Brown Rice Mix   *Serves 4*

Rice and wholewheat mix may be served in place of either rice or wholewheat alone.

4 oz (100 g) wholewheat, soaked overnight
8 oz (225 g) brown rice

2 pt (1·1 litres) water
½ teaspoon salt

Place all ingredients in a heavy saucepan and bring to the boil. Reduce the heat and simmer for 1½ hours. The rice will be very soft in contrast to the chewy wheat.

Wholewheat Pilau   *Serves 4*

8 oz (225 g) wholewheat, soaked and drained
4 tablespoons vegetable oil
1 medium onion, chopped
2–3 cloves garlic, crushed
3 sticks celery, chopped
1 pt (575 ml) hot water

2 oz (50 g) sultanas
4 oz (100 g) mushrooms, sliced
4 oz (100 g) unsalted peanuts
1 teaspoon nutmeg
1 teaspoon ground ginger
salt and black pepper to taste

Fry the wheat in oil in a heavy pan for 5 minutes. Add the onion, garlic and celery and cook for another 5 minutes. Add the water, sultanas and mushrooms. Cover and simmer until all the liquid is absorbed and the wheat is just tender (about 45 minutes to 1 hour). You may need to add more water if the wheat is not cooked. Stir in the rest of the ingredients and adjust the seasoning as necessary. Serve immediately.

Bulgar wheat

Bulgar, also known as burghul and cracked wheat, is still something of a mystery in the West, although nowadays it can be bought in most wholefood shops. It is a wheat product that from ancient times has been made in parts of Western Asia; Eastern Europe and North Africa. It has excellent nutritional qualities, a fine taste and lends itself to many ways of cooking.

Bulgar is prepared by parboiling wholewheat grains in a minimum amount of water. The wheat is then spread thinly on a cloth or tray, dried out (traditionally in the sun) and finally cracked between stone rollers. The starch in the grain is gelatinized by the boiling water and after drying and cracking this results in a hard, vitreous product. The boiling process also has the affect of diffusing part of the wheat germ and bran into the starchy centre of the wheat and if the wheat is then cracked or milled the product retains almost all the goodness of the whole grain.

Bulgar wheat is cooked by steaming or boiling, and sometimes it is dry roasted first. It can be bought in various grades ranging from fine to coarsely cracked. Sometimes the makers parboil and roast the bulgar, before packaging it, to give a fast cooking product.

Bulgar may be served instead of rice with meat, vegetables or sauces, or as the basis for a cold salad (see index for tabbouleh or bazargan recipes). The methods given below prepare enough bulgar for 3 to 4 servings.

Boiled Bulgar Wheat   *Serves 3–4*

Method 1

8 oz (225 g) bulgar wheat
16 fl oz (450 ml) water
salt to taste

Dry roast the bulgar in a heavy saucepan over a medium heat for 2 to 3 minutes stirring constantly. Remove from the heat, allow to cool for a couple of minutes and then add the water. Bring to the boil, reduce the heat, cover and simmer for 15 to 20 minutes or until all the water is absorbed. Salt to taste towards the end of cooking time.

Method 2

2 tablespoons vegetable oil
1 clove garlic, crushed
8 oz (225 g) bulgar wheat

16 fl oz (450 ml) water *or* stock
salt, black pepper and cayenne to
  taste

Heat the oil in a heavy pan and lightly sauté the garlic. Add the bulgar and gently fry, stirring, for 2 to 3 minutes. Pour in the stock or water and simmer over a very low heat for 15 to 20 minutes or until all the water is absorbed. Towards the end of cooking time season to taste with salt, pepper and cayenne.

Pine nuts make a really delicious addition to bulgar. Fry 1 oz (25 g) pine nuts in the oil along with the garlic and then proceed with the recipe as directed.

Method 3

2 tablespoons vegetable oil
1 medium onion, finely chopped
8 oz (225 g) bulgar
16 fl oz (450 ml) boiling water
salt to taste

Heat the oil in a heavy pan over a high heat, add the onion and sauté until just browned. Reduce the heat and pour in the bulgar and boiling water. Stir well, add salt to taste, cover and cook over a low heat until all the water is absorbed (15 to 20 minutes).

Bulgar Wheat Gratin   *Serves 4*

8 oz (225 g) bulgar wheat
16 fl oz (450 ml) water *or* vegetable
  stock
salt, black pepper and cayenne to
  taste
2 tablespoons vegetable oil
1 medium onion, diced

1 medium green pepper, cored,
  seeded and diced
4 oz (100 g) mushrooms, sliced
8 fl oz (225 ml) béchamel sauce
  (see index)
4 oz (100 g) cheese, grated

Preheat the oven to 375°F (190°C, gas mark 5). Cook the bulgar wheat using Method 1 (above). Meanwhile heat the oil in a heavy pan, sauté the onion and green pepper until just soft, stir in the mushrooms and cook for a further 2 to 3 minutes. Prepare béchamel sauce. Place the bulgar wheat in a casserole dish, cover it with the onion, pepper and mushroom mixture, pour the béchamel sauce over the dish, sprinkle grated cheese and bake uncovered in the preheated oven for 30 minutes or until nicely browned.

Pasta

Pasta is made from a dough of flour, eggs and water. The dough is rolled out and cut into any of a huge variety of shapes, then dried before cooking in water. The best pasta is made from hard-grained wheats, particularly durum wheat. Wholemeal flour makes good pasta but the dough is harder to roll out thinly than one made from white flour. A dough made from a combination of flours is both nutritious and easy to work with. The dough can be mixed by hand or in a food processor. The rolling out requires time and patience and if you eat a lot of pasta it may be worth buying a domestic size, hand-operated rolling and cutting machine.

Wholemeal Pasta   *Serves 4*

8 oz (225 g) strong white flour
8 oz (225 g) wholemeal flour
1 teaspoon salt
3 large eggs
2–3 tablespoons water

To make the dough with a food processor put the flours and salt in the bowl of the machine and add the eggs. Process until the mixture has the texture of moist breadcrumbs. Leave the machine running and add the water slowly until the dough forms a ball. Do not add any more water. Process the dough until it feels elastic. It is now ready to roll out. To make the dough by hand put the flours into a mixing bowl. Beat the eggs together with the salt and add them to the flour. Work them into the flour until, again, you have a mixture that has the texture of moist breadcrumbs. Add the water very slowly until the dough sticks together and forms a ball. Stop adding the water. Knead the dough for 5 to 10 minutes until it is firm and elastic. Flour the dough and leave it to rest for 20 minutes.

Shaping the Pasta

Flour a large board or work surface. Cut the dough into two pieces and shape one piece into a thick sausage. With a floured rolling pin, roll the dough out lengthwise starting from the middle of the sausage and rolling centre left and then centre right. The intention is to produce a sheet of dough about 18 in (45 cm) long, rectangular in shape and as thin as you can make it. The process is not easy and it requires patience and practice. Repeat for the other piece of dough. Now cut the pastry sheets into whatever shape you require. For cannelloni shells cut the sheets into 4 in (10 cm) squares, for lasagne into 4 in × 10 in (10 cm × 25 cm) rectangles, for tagliatelle roll the pastry sheet up like a roll of lino and cut slices ¼ in (5 mm) thick off the end with a sharp knife. If you are using the pasta the same day leave it to dry on a floured board until needed. Otherwise deep freeze it while still moist or leave it to dry out completely and then store it in the refrigerator in a sealed plastic bag or container.

Cooking pasta

The important rule when cooking pasta is to use a large pot and plenty of water. Generally 1 lb (450 g) pasta needs 6 pints (3 litres) water. For salt, 1½ tablespoons per 1 lb (450 g) pasta is an average amount, added after the water has boiled and before the pasta is put in. To prevent the pasta sticking to itself during cooking, a little butter or oil is added to the water. Thus, the water is brought to a rolling boil, salted, about 2 tablespoons oil are added and the pasta is then carefully fed into the pot and boiled, uncovered, until it is soft on the outside but with a slight resistance at the centre i.e. *al dente*. Cooking times vary depending on the type of pasta, and whether it is bought or home-made. Shop-bought pasta will have cooking times on the packet. Fresh home-made pasta requires 5 to 7 minutes. As soon as the pasta is cooked, drain it in a colander and serve.

Serve pasta with a sauce and grated cheese or on its own dressed with melted butter or olive oil and seasoned with freshly milled black pepper.

Note: Wholemeal pasta is more nutritious and is higher in protein than normal white flour pasta.

Lasagne Verdi   *Serves 4*

Make the pasta as directed above but add 3 oz (75 g) cooked, drained spinach purée to the dough at the same time as the eggs. Reduce the amount of water used to obtain a firm dough. Roll out as directed for lasagne.

Boiled Noodles   *Serves 4*

1 lb (450 g) dried noodles   1 tablespoon salt
6 pt (3·4 litres) water   2 tablespoons vegetable oil

Bring the water to the boil, add the salt, oil and noodles and stir gently. Cook the noodles, uncovered, in gently boiling water until they are soft on the outside with a slight resistance at the core (about 5 minutes). Drain the noodles and if they are not to be used immediately, rinse them under cold running water, then drain them and stir in a little oil to stop them sticking together. To reheat, pour boiling water over the noodles.

Fried Noodles

There are two ways of frying noodles: soft frying in a little oil or deep drying. In each case the noodles are pre-cooked, drained and cooled before frying.

To soft fry noodles, heat 2 to 3 tablespoons oil per 8 oz (225 g) cooked noodles, in a heavy frying pan. Add the noodles and sauté with constant stirring for 4 to 5 minutes. To deep fry, separate the cooked noodles into single strands, fill a heavy pan or deep frying pan with 3 to 4 in (7 to 10 cm) oil and heat it to 350°F (180°C). Drop in the noodles, a handful at a time, and fry until medium brown in colour. Remove with chopsticks and drain on absorbent paper.

Rice

The cooking qualities of rice differ considerably depending on the source of the rice, its age and whether it is long or short grain, but the following general rules are useful:

1. 8 oz (225 g) uncooked rice gives about 1½ lb (700 g) cooked rice.
2. 1 volume uncooked rice gives 3 volumes cooked rice.
3. 2–3 oz (50–75 g) uncooked rice per person is an average serving.
4. 1 volume of uncooked rice requires 2 volumes of water to cook in.

The nutritional merits of using brown rice rather than white rice are discussed in Section 4. Washing rice causes a loss of nutrients and European or American packed white rice requires only light rinsing before cooking. Asian packed or loose rice and brown rice should be well rinsed. If the rice has been rinsed before cooking it is not necessary to do so again afterwards. The recipes given here do not stipulate long or short grain rice since cooking methods and times are about the same for both.

Brown Rice   *Serves 4*

12 oz (350 g) brown rice
1¼ pt (700 ml) water
½ teaspoon salt

Method 1: boiled

Wash the rice thoroughly in cold water. Drain and transfer it to a heavy pot, add the water and bring to the boil. Add the salt, cover the pot, reduce the heat and simmer for 50 minutes. Remove the pot from the heat and allow it to stand for 10 minutes. Mix the rice gently with a wooden spoon or rice paddle and serve.

Method 2: pressure-cooked

Wash the rice thoroughly in cold water. Drain and transfer it to a pressure cooker. Cover and bring to full pressure over a high heat. Reduce the heat to very low and gently simmer for 12 to 15 minutes. Remove the pressure cooker from the heat, allow the pressure to drop to normal, uncover it, add the salt, gently mix the rice with a wooden spoon or rice paddle, cover the cooker again and allow the rice to stand for 5 minutes before serving.

Method 3: baked

Preheat the oven to 350°F (180°C, gas mark 4). Wash the rice thoroughly in cold water and drain well. Place the rice in a heavy frying pan and dry roast it over a medium heat until the rice is dry, deeper in colour and beginning to pop. Transfer it to a casserole dish, add the water, boiling, and salt, cover and bake in the preheated oven for 50 to 60 minutes. Mix the cooked rice gently with a wooden spoon or rice paddle and serve.

Boiled White Rice   *Serves 4*

1¼ pt (700 ml) water
½ teaspoon salt
12 oz (350 g) white rice

Bring the water to the boil in a heavy saucepan. Toss in the salt and add the rice. Return to the boil, reduce the heat, cover and simmer for 15 to 20 minutes or until the rice is puffed up, dry and just tender (exact times will depend on the type of rice).

Simple Fried Rice   *Serves 4*

This well-known Chinese dish is a really excellent way of using up any leftover rice or vegetables. It's best cooked very fast in a wok, but if you haven't got one use a large, heavy frying pan over a high heat.

2 tablespoons vegetable oil
1 lb (450 g) cooked rice (white or
   brown)
2 eggs, beaten
2–3 spring onions, chopped
soy sauce

Heat the oil in a heavy frying pan or wok over a high heat. Put the rice in the pan and stir fry for 2 to 3 minutes. Reduce the heat and pour in the eggs. Stir fry for 4 to 5 minutes. Transfer from the pan to a serving dish, sprinkle the spring onions and soy sauce over the top. Serve.

Red Rice   *Serves 4*

Rice and aduki beans eaten together provide a rich protein source as well as a colourful dish.

4 oz (100 g) aduki beans, soaked in
   water for 6 hours or more
2 pt (1·1 litres) water
1 lb (450 g) brown rice, washed,
   drained
1 teaspoon salt
2 tablespoons sesame seeds, toasted

Drain the soaked beans. Place them in the pot with the water, bring them to the boil, reduce the heat, then cover and simmer until cooked (about 1½ hours). Drain and reserve the liquid. Put the rice in the pot, add more water to the bean cooking liquid to make 1½ pints (850 ml) and add to the rice. Cover and bring to the boil. Reduce the heat and simmer, covered, for 30 minutes. Now add the beans, mix well and continue to simmer until the rice is cooked (about 20 minutes). Combine the salt and toasted sesame seeds. Serve the red rice hot or cold, garnished with the sesame seed and salt mixture (a Japanese condiment known as *gomashio*).

Basic Rice Pilau   *Serves 4*

4 tablespoons vegetable oil
2 large onions, finely diced
2 oz (50 g) pine nuts *or* almonds
1 lb (450 g) long grain brown rice
½ teaspoon mixed spice
1 teaspoon dried sage
1 tablespoon parsley, finely
   chopped *or* 1 teaspoon dried
   parsley

salt and black pepper to taste
2 oz (50 g) sultanas *or* raisins
2 medium tomatoes, quartered
1½ pt (850 ml) boiling water *or*
   vegetable stock

In a large heavy saucepan heat the oil and sauté the onions until soft, but not brown. Add the pine nuts or almonds and rice and fry, stirring, for 4–5 minutes. Add the mixed spice, sage, parsley and season to taste with salt and freshly milled black pepper. Stir in the sultanas or raisins and tomatoes and then pour in the water or stock. Stir well, bring to the boil, reduce the heat, cover and simmer until all the liquid is absorbed (45 to 50 minutes). Leave the pilau covered, away from the heat, for 10 minutes and then serve.

Corn

Corn on the Cob   *Serves 4*

Buy the freshest corn you can. To test for freshness press one of the kernels: if it spurts juice it's fresh.

Method 1: boiled

The following recipe gives the simplest and one of the best ways of preparing corn on the cob. Serve the corn with a good size knob of butter.

4 ears of corn
water
salt
pinch basil (optional)
butter

If the corn hasn't already been stripped, remove the husks and silk. (To remove the silk, hold the ear of corn under a cold running tap and brush with a soft vegetable brush.) Bring a large pan of water to the boil (there should be enough water to just cover all the ears of corn), add a pinch of salt and basil, and then drop in the corn. Return the water to the boil and cook the corn for 4 to 6 minutes or until tender. Drain and serve with a knob of butter.

Method 2: baked

This method is an excellent way of preparing corn on the cob both at home and out-of-doors on camping trips or at a barbeque when a wood fire or charcoal grill is used in place of the oven.

4 ears of corn in husks
1 tablespoon vegetable oil *or*
    melted butter
salt to taste

Preheat the oven to 425°F (220°C, gas mark 7). Open the ears of corn by gently turning back the husks. Remove the silk and then brush each ear with oil or butter, and sprinkle with salt to taste. Replace the husks, place the cobs on a baking tray and bake in the preheated oven until tender (about 15 minutes). To cook on a fire, allow the flames to die down and place the corn cobs, prepared as above, on the hot embers. Keep turning them and bake for 15 to 20 minutes.

Spiked Corn Casserole   *Serves 4*

A spicy and nutritious corn dish.

2 tablespoons vegetable oil
1 clove garlic, crushed
1 medium onion, diced
3 large ripe tomatoes, chopped
  or 8 oz (225 g) tinned tomatoes,
  chopped
1 small chilli pepper, chopped
  or ½ teaspoon hot pepper sauce

1 lb (450 g) fresh corn, cut from the
  cobs or 1 lb (450 g) tinned
  or frozen corn
salt and black pepper to taste
8 fl oz (225 ml) milk

Heat the oil in a heavy pan, add the garlic and onion and sauté until golden. Add the tomatoes, chilli and fresh corn (add the tinned corn, if used, later), mix well, reduce the heat and cook, stirring, for 10 minutes. Now season to taste with salt and black pepper, pour in the milk (and tinned corn) and cover. Reduce the heat to low and simmer for 20 to 25 minutes.

Oats

Porridge   *Serves 4*

A great deal has been written about the preparation of this apparently simple dish; probably as many different ways of making it have been recommended as there are Scots. One interesting idea is that porridge should be made by gradually adding pinches of uncooked oatmeal to the pot as the porridge boils, so that when the dish is ready it contains a range of textures, from completely cooked to raw oatmeal. This is perhaps a method to experiment with.

There are two main things to remember when making porridge. Firstly, do not add the salt until the oatmeal is well swollen otherwise the salt hardens the meal and prevents proper swelling. Secondly, use a heavy pot and a long cooking time over a very low heat.

1 pt (575 ml) water
4 oz (100 g) rolled oats
salt to taste
cold cream or milk

Bring the water to the boil in a pot and slowly sprinkle in the oatmeal with one hand whilst stirring briskly with a wooden spoon with the other. Return the pot to the boil, reduce the heat to a very low simmer and cook for 20 minutes, then season to taste with salt. Cover again and cook for a further 10 minutes. Stir occasionally during cooking. Serve with milk or cream. Traditionally the milk or cream is served in individual bowls and each spoonful of hot porridge is dipped into it before being eaten.

Variations:

Serve with honey or sugar and dried or fresh fruit.

Muesli   *Serves 1*

Muesli was formulated by Dr Bircher-Benner over seventy years ago. He was a well-known, if slightly off-beat, nutritionist who founded a famous health clinic in Zurich. His recipe for muesli included a mixture of oats, raw fruits, nuts and milk. Although intended as a food for any time of day, this combination and its derivatives have since become regarded as a breakfast cereal. The recipe was devised to provide a food that supplied good amounts of protein, vitamins, minerals and roughage without overloading the body with too much rich food. His ideas were well ahead of his time and now many of them are supported by medical opinion. Muesli is considered by most nutritionists to be an excellent food combination.

2–3 level tablespoons rolled oats
1 eating apple, grated
1 teaspoon fresh lemon juice
2 level tablespoons natural low fat
   yoghurt

1 level tablespoon roasted,
   chopped nuts
milk *or* cream to taste
honey *or* brown sugar to taste

Grate the apple just before it's needed and then combine it with the oats, lemon juice and yoghurt. Sprinkle nuts over the top and add milk and honey to taste.

Variations:

1. Use dried fruit, soaked overnight, or another fresh fruit in place of apple.
2. Soak the oats overnight in milk. Muesli prepared this way is softer in texture and more digestible for some people.

High-Energy Oat Cereal   *8–10 Servings*

This is a breakfast cereal designed to help you start the day full of energy. Make more than you need and store the rest in an airtight tin.

1 lb (450 g) quick-cooking rolled
  oats
2 oz (50 g) dried apricots, chopped
2 oz (50 g) dates, chopped

4 oz (100 g) sunflower seeds
2 oz (50 g) raisins
4 oz (100 g) mixed roasted nuts

Combine all the ingredients and serve portions of the mixture with milk, honey and chopped banana.

High Protein Breakfast Cereal   *8–10 Servings*

This is a protein-rich breakfast food. Make more than you need and store the rest for later use.

6 oz (175 g) rolled oats
4 oz (100 g) soya flour
2 tablespoons bran
3 tablespoons wheat germ
2 oz (50 g) brown sugar

4 fl oz (100 ml) vegetable oil
1 oz (25 g) sesame seeds, toasted
1 oz (25 g) sunflower seeds, toasted
4 oz (100 g) raisins *or* sultanas

Preheat the oven to 325°F (170°C, gas mark 3). Combine all the ingredients except the sesame and sunflower seeds and the raisins or sultanas. Mix well and spread the mixture on a shallow baking tray or dish. Place in the preheated oven on a tray and roast for 40 minutes, stirring twice during this time. Remove from the oven, stir in the seeds and raisins or sultanas and use as required. Store unused cereal in screwtop jars in the refrigerator.

Oat and Herb Rissoles   *Serves 4*

16 fl oz (450 ml) water
4 oz (100 g) rolled oats
1 medium onion, finely chopped
1 teaspoon dried mixed herbs
1 teaspoon dried basil
1 tablespoon soy sauce

1 tablespoon tomato purée
salt and pepper to taste
2 eggs, beaten
wholemeal flour
wholemeal breadcrumbs for coating
vegetable oil for shallow frying

Bring the water to the boil and stir in the oats. Cook for 15 minutes, stirring frequently. Add the onion, herbs and sauces. Season to taste with salt and black pepper. Add half the beaten egg and enough flour to make a stiff dough. Flour hands and roll the mixture into small rissoles, dip them into the remaining beaten egg and then roll them in the breadcrumbs. Now shallow fry until they are golden brown on both sides.

Barley

The recipes stipulate whole barley kernels. Pearl barley, which is more generally available, is only suitable for making soups, puddings and barley water. Cooked whole barley can be used much as you would use rice.

Plain Barley   *Serves 4*

8 oz (225 g) whole barley
1¼ pt (700 ml) water
salt to taste

Combine the ingredients in a heavy saucepan and bring to the boil. Reduce the heat, cover and simmer for 50 minutes or until the barley is cooked.

Toasted Barley (boiled)   *Serves 4*

8 oz (225 g) whole barley
1¼ pt (700 ml) water
salt to taste

Place the barley in a heavy pot and dry roast over a high heat, stirring constantly, until the barley darkens to a deep brown colour. Remove the pan from the heat and carefully add the water, taking care it does not splutter on you. Salt to taste, bring to the boil, reduce the heat, cover and simmer for 40 minutes or until the barley is cooked.

Barley Pilau   *Serves 4*

4 oz (100 g) vegetable oil
8 oz (225 g) mushrooms, chopped
1 medium onion, sliced
1 medium green pepper, cored,
  seeded and sliced
8 oz (225 g) whole barley

1 clove garlic, crushed
1¼ pt (700 ml) vegetable stock
  or water
1 teaspoon dried thyme
salt and black pepper to taste

Preheat the oven to 350°F (180°C, gas mark 4). Heat the oil in a frying pan and sauté the mushrooms until well softened. Transfer the mushrooms to a greased casserole dish. Sauté the onion and green pepper in the frying pan until the onion softens and lightly browns. Transfer the mixture to the casserole dish. Put the barley into the frying pan and stir fry, coating each grain in oil. Add the garlic and pour the stock over the barley. Heat to boiling. Transfer this mixture to the casserole, add the thyme, stir well and season to taste with salt and black pepper. Cover and bake in the preheated oven for 40 minutes or until the barley is tender.

Lentil and Barley Rissoles   *Serves 4*

1 lb (450 g) cooked, drained whole barley
8 oz (225 g) cooked, drained, split red lentils
4 oz (100 g) cheese, grated
1 egg, beaten

1 tablespoon tomato purée
1 teaspoon salt
½ teaspoon black pepper
½ teaspoon dried thyme
about 2 oz (50 g) wholemeal flour
oil for shallow frying

Combine all the ingredients (except the oil), adding enough flour to form a mixture of such consistency that it will hold its shape. Wet your hands and form the mixture into oval rissoles 3 in (7.5 cm) long. Shallow fry them until they are golden brown on both sides.

Barley Water

Serve this refreshing drink cold in the summer or hot in winter months.

2 oz (50 g) whole barley, rinsed
2 pt (1·1 litres) boiling water
2 strips lemon rind

juice of 1 lemon
sugar to taste

Place the barley in the top of a double boiler or in a heavy pan. Add the boiling water and lemon rind and juice. Cover and simmer for 2 hours. Strain, sweeten to taste. Serve hot or chilled.

Millet
Plain Millet   *Serves 4*

Method 1

1 pt (550 ml) water
½ teaspoon salt
8 oz (225 g) millet

Bring the water to the boil in a heavy pan with a good, tight-fitting lid. Add the salt and millet, stir and return to the boil. Cover, reduce the heat and simmer for about 35 to 40 minutes or until all the water is absorbed and the millet is tender.

Method 2

This method requires a little more trouble than Method 1 but it brings out the natural flavour of the grain.

2 teaspoons vegetable oil
8 oz (225 g) millet

1¼ pt (700 ml) water
½ teaspoon salt

Coat the bottom of a heavy saucepan with the oil and heat it over a medium flame. Add the millet and sauté, stirring constantly, until it is lightly browned. Allow the pan to cool a little and then stir in the water. Add the salt, bring to the boil, cover, reduce the heat and simmer for 40 minutes or until all the water is absorbed and the millet is tender.

Millet with Cheese   *Serves 4*

8 oz (225 g) millet
1 pt (575 ml) vegetable stock
  or water

salt to taste
2 tablespoons vegetable oil
8 oz (225 g) cheese, grated

Put the millet in a heavy saucepan, add the stock (or water) and salt to taste and bring to the boil. Cover, reduce the heat and simmer for 35 to 40 minutes. Stir in the oil and half the cheese and keep stirring until the cheese melts. Pour the mixture into a serving dish, top with the remaining cheese and serve.

Rye

Plain Rye   *Serves 4*

8 oz (225 g) whole rye, covered in
  water and soaked overnight
1 pt (575 ml) water
½ teaspoon salt

Drain the rye and put it into a heavy saucepan. Add the water and bring to the boil. Stir in the salt, cover and reduce the heat to very low. Simmer for one hour or until rye is tender.

Substitute cooked whole rye for brown rice or wholewheat either as a side dish or as an ingredient in savoury dishes such as pilaus, risottos, etc.

Rye Porridge   *Serves 4*

8 oz (225 g) rye flakes
1¼ pt (700 ml) water
½ teaspoon salt

milk, honey, fresh fruit, etc. to
   accompany porridge

Put the rye and water into a heavy pot and bring to the boil. Add the salt and mix well. Cover, reduce the heat to a minimum and simmer for about 40 minutes, stirring occasionally. This makes quite a thick porridge. For a thinner, creamier porridge use more water and a longer cooking time. Serve with honey, milk or fresh fruit to taste.

Buckwheat

If the buckwheat you buy is preroasted (brown in colour) use either Method 1 or 2. If it is unroasted (pale in colour) use Method 2.

Plain Buckwheat (Kasha)   *Serves 3–4*

Method 1

8 oz (225 g) buckwheat
16 fl oz (450 ml) boiling water
½ teaspoon salt
2 oz (50 g) melted butter

Toast the buckwheat in a heavy, dry saucepan over a medium heat until it turns a deep colour and starts to smell nutty. Stir constantly to prevent it from burning. Pour the boiling water over, add the salt and cover. Reduce the heat and simmer for 15 to 20 minutes or until all the water has been absorbed and the buckwheat is tender.

Method 2

2 teaspoons sesame oil
8 oz (225 g) buckwheat
16 fl oz (450 ml) boiling water
pinch of salt

Heat the oil in a heavy pan over a medium heat. Add the buckwheat and stir fry for about 3 minutes. Pour the boiling water in, add some salt and cover. Reduce the heat and simmer for 15 minutes. Remove from the heat and allow to stand for 5 minutes. Serve.

Kasha Croquettes   *Serves 4*

1 lb (450 g) cooked buckwheat
2 oz (50 g) wholewheat flour
1 onion, finely diced
4 oz (100 g) cooked vegetables
  or cooked beans, finely diced

1 tablespoon soy sauce
water
oil for frying

Combine the first five ingredients and mix in enough water (if needed) to form a firm mixture that will hold its shape. Form this mixture into balls about 2 in (5 cm) in diameter or into burger shapes. Deep fry the balls in hot oil until golden brown or shallow fry the burgers in a little oil in a heavy frying pan. Brown both sides.

Pulses

Beans, peas and lentils, collectively called pulses, are a rich source of protein, carbohydrate and some vitamins and minerals. Correctly soaked and cooked, pulses are easily digested and, in this section, detailed cooking instructions are given, plus tips on buying.

Beans, peas and lentils cooked on their own can be used in salads, soups and stuffings, or puréed to make dips and spreads. Mixed with cooked grains they make a particularly nutritious combination. More elaborate dishes containing one of the pulses as a main ingredient are given in the high-protein recipes.

Buying pulses

Buy your pulses, if possible, from a reputable and busy health or wholefood store since, although beans can be stored for very long periods, if they get really old they take longer to cook and taste tough. Also some sacks of beans, particularly lentils, contain more small stones and grit than others, and these are to be avoided if you want to escape the tedious task of picking over the beans before cooking them. You may avoid the problem altogether by buying pre-packed beans from a supermarket, but you will probably pay more for them than for the loose variety and also your choice will be limited. Store the beans in airtight containers in a dry, coolish place.

Soaking pulses

Nearly all beans and peas must be soaked before cooking to ensure they are digestible. This long soaking does require you to remember to do it in advance of the meal. The usual soaking times are 12 to 24 hours although there is a quicker soaking method (discussed below). Strictly speaking, lentils and split peas do not require soaking but if you do soak them it doesn't do any harm and speeds up the cooking time.

Long soaking method

Weigh out the beans you require (8 oz/225 g serves about 4 people) and pick over them to remove any grit or stones or odd looking beans. Cover the beans in water (1½ pints/850 ml water per 8 oz/225 g beans). Leave them according to the recommended soaking times given in the chart (below). If the beans are cooked in the water they were soaked in, then usually by the end of the cooking time the water is almost completely absorbed and the beans do not need to be drained. This method means that any vitamins lost into the water are regained. Of course more water may be added during cooking if necessary. If you forget or need to leave the beans longer than the recommended soaking time, then they should be drained and covered with fresh water before cooking.

Quick soaking method

In a heavy saucepan, weigh out the beans and cover with water as directed in the long soaking method. Cover the pot and bring to the boil, reduce the heat and simmer for 5 minutes. Remove the pot from the heat and leave the beans to soak for the quick-method time given in the chart (below). After this time bring the beans back to the boil in the same water and cook until tender. Cooking times are the same as for the long soaking method.

Cooking pulses

Times

There are two schools of thought on whether beans should be cooked for a long time without pressure or for a short time under pressure in a pressure cooker. The pressure-cook faction claim their method saves on fuel, time and labour and also increases the digestibility of the beans. The long-cooking lobby claim that fast cooking results in beans crumbly on the outside and hard inside. Further, they claim that it is very difficult to gauge exactly how long a particular type of bean will take to cook and that it is inadvisable to keep cooling down the pressure cooker while checking. Also it's not possible to add ingredients during the cooking process, and not possible to remove any scum that forms.

My preference is for the long cooking method. Once the beans are on, cooking, they can be forgotten about except for the occasional look. Seasoning and herbs can be adjusted as you feel necessary and the tastes of other ingredients have much longer to mingle and merge together with that of the beans. From my experience, long soaking and slow cooking produce the tastiest bean dishes and those least likely to give problems with flatulence later.

Soaking and Cooking Time for Various Pulses

Type of pulse	Soaking times		Cooking times
	long method	short method	
Aduki beans	2 to 3 hours	1 hour	1–1½ hours
Black beans	overnight*	3 hours	1½–2 hours
Black-eyed beans	overnight*	2 hours	1–1½ hours
Broad beans	overnight*	4 hours	1½–2 hours
Lima/butter beans	overnight*	4 hours	1½–2 hours
Chickpeas	overnight*	3 hours	1½–2 hours
Kidney beans including:			
Barlotti	overnight*	2–3 hours	1–1½ hours
Canellini	overnight*	2–3 hours	1–1½ hours
Dutch brown bean	overnight*	2–3 hours	1½–2 hours
Egyptian brown bean (ful medames)	overnight*	2–3 hours	1½–2 hours
Fagioli	overnight*	2–3 hours	1–1½ hours
Field bean	overnight*	2–3 hours	1–1½ hours
Flageolets	overnight*	2–3 hours	1–1½ hours
Great northern bean	overnight*	2–3 hours	1½–2 hours
Haricot beans	overnight*	2–3 hours	1½–2 hours
Navy bean	overnight*	2–3 hours	1–1½ hours
Pink bean	overnight*	2–3 hours	1–1½ hours
Pinto bean	overnight*	2–3 hours	1–1½ hours
Pearl bean	overnight*	2–3 hours	1–1½ hours
Red kidney bean	overnight*	2–3 hours	1–1½ hours
White bean	overnight*	2–3 hours	1–1½ hours
Lentils	no soaking needed		small lentils: 20–30 minutes large lentils: 35–40 minutes
Mung beans	overnight*	45–60 minutes	45 minutes
Pigeon peas	overnight*	2 hours	1 hour
Peas	overnight*	2 hours	1 hour
Split peas	no soaking needed		20–30 minutes
Soya beans	24 hours	do not use this method	3–4 hours

Tips

1. Do not add salt to the beans until near the end of the cooking time otherwise they harden and take longer to cook.
2. Other seasonings should be added later as well as beans, while cooking, seem to absorb and neutralize flavours. Lentils and split peas are the exception to this rule and can be seasoned at the start of cooking.
3. If a bean dish is to be reheated the following day check the seasoning and add more before serving if necessary.
4. Do not add bicarbonate of soda to the cooking water. It's not needed and destroys vitamins.
5. Water in which beans have been cooked makes excellent stock.

* 'overnight' means 8 to 12 hours

6. Chickpeas and red beans tend to foam when first cooked; remove the scum after 20 to 30 minutes and again later if any more forms.
7. Cook twice as many beans as you need and store the extra in the fridge until needed. I find they keep best if only lightly covered. They will keep for four to five days. Use for making soups, salads, spreads and dips; mashed for rissoles; combined with cooked grains; as an accompaniment to a main meal.
8. One volume of dried beans gives 2 to 2½ volumes of cooked beans, and one weight of dried beans gives 2 to 2½ weights of cooked beans.

Nuts

Nuts are a concentrated source of proteins, vitamins, minerals, fats and fibre. Add them to salads, soups, cooked grains and main meals, or eat them on their own as a snack. Nuts can also be crushed to make spreads and butters. This section deals with preparing nuts for a variety of uses.

Shelling, blanching and skinning nuts

Almonds

These nuts can sometimes be shelled with a twist of the fingers otherwise, if the shell is too hard, a sharp tap with a hammer is normally enough to break it. To remove the brown skin from the nut itself, drop the nuts into boiling water for 5 minutes, drain, rinse in cold water and the skin will just slip off.

Brazil nuts

Most easily shelled after being chilled in the refrigerator for a day or two. Use a nut cracker or small hammer.

Chestnuts

Easier to shell and skin after boiling or roasting. Cut 2 slits in the outer casing on the flat side of each of the nuts and drop them in boiling water for 2 to 3 minutes. Drain and leave them to cool. The casing and skin can now be removed with a vegetable knife. Alternatively place the slit chestnuts on a baking tray in a hot oven and cook for 10 minutes or until the slits start to open up. Remove them from the oven and the casing and skin can be easily removed with the help of a knife. Otherwise you may wish to buy ready peeled, dried chestnuts from a Chinese store or delicatessen. To reconstitute, cover the chestnuts with water and soak overnight.

Hazelnuts, cobnuts and filberts

These can be shelled by hitting the centre of the rounded side of the nut with a light hammer. To skin the nuts bake them in a moderate oven for 10 to 15 minutes, allow them to cool and then, if the nuts are rolled in a damp cloth, the skin will just slip off. Otherwise drop them into a pan of boiling water and leave them to stand for 5 to 10 minutes. Drain, rinse in cold water and rub off the skins.

Walnuts

These nuts can be shelled by striking the junction of the two halves with a light hammer.

Chopping, slicing and grinding nuts

For coarsely chopped nuts, place them in an electric grinder and switch the machine on for just a few seconds. Leave it longer to grind or mill the nuts completely. Otherwise put the nuts in a wooden bowl and chop them with a sharp vegetable knife; for fine grinding use a pestle and mortar. To slice nuts, use a sharp knife and slice each one individually. If the nuts are very hard try boiling them first, for a couple of minutes.

Roasting nuts and seeds

Preheat the oven to 325°F (170°C, gas mark 3). Spread the whole or chopped nuts or seeds on a baking tray and place them in the oven. Bake them for about 10 minutes giving them a shake once or twice during this time. The nuts or seeds are ready when lightly browned. Nuts or seeds may also be pan roasted on top of the oven. Put them in an ungreased, heavy frying pan and gently toss them about over a moderate flame until lightly browned.

For spiced roasted nuts sprinkle the roasting nuts with the following ingredients, well mixed, just before you remove them from the pan or oven. These amounts will do for 1 lb (450g) of nuts.

2 teaspoons salt
½ teaspoon ground cumin
½ teaspoon ground cinnamon
½ teaspoon ground ginger
½ teaspoon ground cloves
1 tablespoon brown sugar (optional)

Part Three:
Protein Recipes

Main Dishes

Dishes containing dairy produce or nuts

Cheddar Cheese and Brown Rice Bake *Serves 4*

4 eggs, beaten
6 fl oz (175 ml) milk
1 lb (450 g) cooked long grain
  brown rice (8 oz/225 g raw rice)
8 oz (225 g) Cheddar cheese, grated

1 medium green pepper, seeded,
  cored and diced
1 medium onion, diced
4 oz (100 g) mushrooms, sliced
salt and pepper to taste

Preheat the oven to 350°F (180°C, gas mark 4). Beat together the egg and milk in a large mixing bowl and stir in the remaining ingredients. Lightly grease a casserole dish and put this mixture into it it. Bake uncovered for 40 minutes or until nicely browned on top and firm in the middle.

Recommended supplementary dish: Basic mixed salad (for recipe see index).

Cheese Rice Cakes *Serves 4*

12 oz (350 g) cooked short grain
  brown rice (6 oz/175 g raw rice)
4 oz (100 g) cheese, finely grated
4 oz (100 g) cottage cheese
1 small onion, finely diced
2 eggs, beaten
1 tablespoon wholemeal flour

$\frac{1}{4}$ teaspoon nutmeg
$\frac{1}{2}$ teaspoon cinnamon
salt and pepper to taste
wholemeal breadcrumbs *or* flour for
  coating
oil for shallow frying

Combine the rice, cheese, onion and half the beaten egg in a mixing bowl and stir well together. Add the flour, nutmeg, cinnamon and salt and pepper to taste. Mix well by hand. Add more flour slowly if the mixture is not firm enough to hold its shape. Shape the mixture into about 10 round cakes. This is easier if you clean your hands after making the mixture and then keep them wet while you shape the cakes. Dip the rice cakes into the remaining beaten egg and roll them in breadcrumbs or flour. Heat the oil in a frying pan and gently fry the rice cakes until nicely browned on both sides (about 5 minutes each side). Keep cooked cakes warm under a low grill whilst frying the remainder.

Recommended supplementary dish: Cauliflower with tahini, lemon and walnut sauce. Cut a small cauliflower into florets and sauté them in 2 tablespoons oil until just softened. Serve smothered with a hot tahini and lemon sauce, with walnuts as a variation (for recipe see index).

Buckwheat Omelette   *Serves 4*

This recipe is from Japan where buckwheat flour is commonly used to make noodles. If buckwheat flour is unavailable you can use wholemeal flour.

4 oz (100 g) buckwheat flour	1 green pepper, seeded, cored and
4 eggs, lightly beaten	diced
4 fl oz (100 ml) water	4 oz (100 g) mushrooms, sliced
1 tablespoon soy sauce	pepper to taste
1 small onion, finely diced	2 tablespoons vegetable oil

Beat the flour, eggs, water and soy sauce into a smooth batter and then stir in the remaining ingredients, except the oil. Heat half the oil in a frying pan and ladle in half the batter mixture. Cook on both sides over a moderate heat until nicely browned. The vegetables should remain slightly crunchy in texture. Repeat for the remaining batter.

Recommended supplementary dish: Protein plus coleslaw salad (for recipe see index).

Rice with Broccoli and Cheese   *Serves 4*

If you wish to prepare the recommended supplementary dish to accompany this meal (see below), prepare it at the same time as the rice with broccoli and cheese, and then they can be baked together.

3 eggs	½ medium onion, chopped
8 fl oz (225 ml) milk	4 oz (100 g) cheese, grated
1 lb (450 g) cooked long grain rice	1 tablespoon tomato purée
(8 oz/225 g raw rice)	½ teaspoon English mustard powder
1 lb (450 g) broccoli, chopped into	salt and black pepper to taste
florets	

Preheat the oven to 350°F (180°C, gas mark 4). Lightly beat together the eggs and milk and then combine the mixture with the remaining ingredients. Put the mixture into a greased baking dish about 8 in (20 cm)×8 in (20 cm) and place the dish in the oven. Bake for 40 minutes or until nicely browned on top and set firm in the middle. The rice with broccoli and cheese will cut into neat squares if allowed to cool a little before serving.

Recommended supplementary dish: Tomatoes with walnut and cottage cheese filling (see recipe below).

Tomatoes with Walnut and Cottage Cheese Filling   *Serves 4*

4 large firm tomatoes
4 oz (100 g) cottage cheese
2 oz (50 g) chopped walnuts
2 oz (50 g) wholemeal breadcrumbs

1 tablespoon freshly diced onion
½ teaspoon dried thyme
salt and black pepper to taste
1 tablespoon vegetable oil

Preheat the oven to 350°F (180°C, gas mark 4). Cut ½-in (1-cm) tops off the tomatoes leaving a ½-in (1-cm) shell. Sprinkle the inside of each shell with a little salt and black pepper. Combine the cottage cheese, walnuts, breadcrumbs, onion, thyme, salt and black pepper and mix well. Stuff the tomatoes with the mixture and press the tops back into place. Brush the tomatoes with oil and put them on a greased baking sheet. Bake in the preheated oven for 30 to 35 minutes.

Vegetable with Potato and Cheese Topping   *Serves 4*

1 lb (450 g) potatoes
6 oz (175 g) Cheddar cheese, grated
1 egg, beaten
2 fl oz (50 ml) milk
salt and freshly milled black pepper
   to taste
2 tablespoons vegetable oil
2 medium onions, finely chopped

2 large carrots, quartered
   lengthwise, and cut thinly across
4 oz (100 g) celery, finely chopped
1 large cooking apple, cored and
   chopped
8 oz (225 g) peanuts
½ teaspoon cayenne
1 teaspoon turmeric

Boil the potatoes in their skins until tender. Drain, rinse them under cold water and peel off the skins. Mash the potatoes and stir in half the cheese, plus the egg and milk and season to taste with salt and black pepper. Beat the mixture smooth. Preheat the oven to 375°F (190°C, gas mark 5). Heat the oil in a large saucepan and add the onions, carrots, celery and apple. Stir well and cook over a medium heat until lightly browned. Add the peanuts, cayenne, turmeric and a little more salt and black pepper and cook, stirring, for a further 1 or 2 minutes.

Put the vegetable mixture into a baking dish and layer the potato and cheese mixture over it. Sprinkle the remaining cheese on the top and bake in the preheated oven for 30 minutes.

Recommended supplementary dish: Bean sprout, beetroot and apple salad (for recipe see index).

Cauliflower with Cheese Sauce and Walnuts   *Serves 4–6*

1 large cauliflower, cut into large
  florets
1 medium onion, finely chopped
1 oz (25 g) wholemeal flour
10 fl oz (275 ml) hot milk
6 oz (175 g) Cheddar cheese, grated

2 teaspoons prepared French
  mustard
salt and black pepper to taste
4 oz (100 g) walnuts, lightly dry
  roasted

Cook the cauliflower in a little water or steam it until tender but still firm. Drain. Melt the butter in a saucepan and sauté the onion until softened. Stir in the flour and then gradually stir in the hot milk. Keep stirring until the sauce has thickened. Add the cheese slowly and finally the mustard and seasoning. Remove the sauce from the heat. Preheat the oven to 350°F (180°C, gas mark 4). Put the cauliflower into a baking dish and pour the cheese sauce over the top. Bake for 15 minutes in the preheated oven. Remove from the oven and top the cauliflower with the walnuts. Continue baking for a further 15 minutes or until the dish has nicely browned.

Recommended supplementary dish: Plain brown rice or bulgar wheat and a basic mixed salad (for recipes see index).

Tortillas with Cheese Filling   *Serves 4*

This dish can be served with or without a tomato sauce.

4 tablespoons vegetable oil
  or melted butter
1 medium onion, finely diced
1 lb (450 g) Cheddar cheese, grated
2 tablespoons finely chopped
  parsley

¼ teaspoon chilli powder
¼ teaspoon ground cumin
salt and black pepper to taste
8 wholemeal tortillas (see page 94
  for recipe, or buy them)
tomato sauce (see page 112), optional

Preheat the oven to 375°F (190°C, gas mark 5). Sauté the onion in half the oil or butter until softened. Combine the cheese, parsley, chilli powder, cumin and seasoning with the onion and the oil it was cooked in. Mix well. Place a line of filling down each tortilla and then fold them over firmly. Place the stuffed tortillas on a greased baking dish and brush the tops with the remaining oil or butter. Now bake them, uncovered, in the preheated oven for 15 to 20 minutes or cover them with tomato sauce and bake them for 25 minutes.

Variations:

Replace part or all of the cheese with the same weight of cooked red kidney beans. Otherwise, kidney beans can be combined with cooked vegetables and/or rice.

Recommended supplementary dish: Mexican red bean salad (for recipe see index).

Parsley Bulgar Wheat Casserole   *Serves 4*

2 tablespoons vegetable oil
2 cloves garlic, crushed
1 medium onion, chopped
1 green pepper, seeded, cored, diced
1 lb (450 g) cooked bulgar wheat

8 oz (225 g) cheese, grated
2 eggs, beaten
10 fl oz (275 ml) milk
1 bunch parsley, finely chopped
½ teaspoon dill seeds
salt and black pepper to taste

Preheat the oven to 350°F (180°C, gas mark 4). Sauté the garlic, onion and green pepper in the oil until softened. Combine the mixture with the remaining ingredients and mix well together. Place in a greased baking dish and bake for 35 minutes or until nicely browned.

Recommended supplementary dishes: Red bean, tomato and onion salad or white bean and beetroot salad (for recipes see index).

Cheese and Nut Balls   *Serves 4*

Serve with tomato sauce (see index) and wholemeal spaghetti.

2 tablespoons vegetable oil
1 medium onion, finely diced
2 cloves garlic, crushed
8 oz (225 g) ground mixed nuts
8 oz (225 g) wholemeal breadcrumbs

4 oz (100 g) cheese, grated
2 teaspoons soy sauce
black pepper to taste
2 eggs, beaten

Sauté the onion and garlic in the oil until softened. Remove them from the heat and stir in the ground nuts and breadcrumbs. Combine the cheese, soy sauce, pepper and beaten eggs and mix well. Stir the nut and cheese mixtures together and mix thoroughly. Preheat the oven to 350°F (180°C, gas mark 4). Form the mixture into 2-in (5-cm) balls (this is easier with wet hands) and place them on a greased baking sheet. Bake for 10 to 12 minutes on one side and then turn the balls over and bake for a further 10 to 12 minutes or until brown and firm. Serve smothered in tomato sauce over wholemeal spaghetti.

Recommended supplementary dish: A basic mixed salad (for recipe see index).

Peanut Burgers   *Makes 4 large burgers*

1 tablespoon vegetable oil
½ medium onion, finely diced
2 oz (50 g) mushrooms, sliced
4 oz (100 g) peanuts, coarsely
　ground
2 oz (50 g) sesame seeds, lightly dry
　roasted
1 oz (25 g) tahini

juice of 1 lemon
2 oz (50 g) wholemeal breadcrumbs
4 oz (100 g) cheese, grated
salt and black pepper to taste
1 egg, beaten
wholemeal flour for coating
oil for shallow frying

Sauté the onion until softened in the oil. Add the mushrooms and sauté for a further minute. Combine this mixture with the peanuts, sesame seeds, tahini, lemon juice, breadcrumbs, cheese and salt and pepper to taste. Stir well and mix thoroughly. Press the mixture into four burgers, brush them with beaten egg and coat with a light sprinkling of wholemeal flour. Fry nicely brown on both sides and serve.

Recommended supplementary dish: Spiced vegetables in yoghurt (see recipe below).

Spiced Vegetables in Yoghurt   *Serves 4*

2 tablespoons vegetable oil
2 medium onions, chopped
2 medium green peppers, seeded,
　cored and chopped
2 medium carrots, cut into
　matchsticks
2 sticks celery, chopped
¼ red dried chilli, seeded and
　chopped *or* ½ teaspoon
　chilli sauce

½ teaspoon ground cumin
½ teaspoon turmeric
¼ teaspoon ground coriander
salt and black pepper to taste
10 fl oz (275 ml) natural low fat
　yoghurt

Heat the oil in a large pan and add the onion, green peppers, carrots and celery. Sauté while stirring over a medium heat until the onion has started to brown. Reduce the heat and stir in the chilli or chilli sauce, cumin, turmeric, coriander and salt and black pepper to taste. Cover the pan and cook with occasional stirring for 5 minutes. Stir in the yoghurt and cook uncovered for a further 5 minutes. The contents should not boil once the yoghurt has been added. The carrots should be tender but still a little crunchy.

Recommended supplementary dish: Serve with peanut burgers (recipe above) or tabbouleh with feta cheese (for recipe see index).

Bistro's Pepperoni Wholemeal Pizza   *Serves 4*

The protein in the pizza bread and the protein in the cheese topping complement one another, making wholemeal pizza an excellent protein source.

Dough
¼ oz (7 g) fresh yeast
1 teaspoon brown sugar
5 fl oz (150 ml) lukewarm water
4 oz (100 g) wholemeal flour
1 teaspoon salt
1 tablespoon vegetable oil

Pizza topping
1 medium onion, sliced thinly
2 oz (50 g) mushrooms, wiped and
    sliced
1 medium green pepper, cored,
    seeded and sliced thinly
8 oz (225 g) Cheddar cheese, grated

Pizza sauce
2 tablespoons olive oil
1 lb (450 g) ripe tomatoes, peeled
    and chopped *or* 14-oz (400-g) can
    peeled tomatoes, chopped
2 tablespoons tomato purée
2 teaspoons fresh oregano, chopped
    or 1 teaspoon dried oregano
salt and pepper

To make the dough

Cream the yeast and sugar together, add the warm water and set aside in a warm place for 15 to 20 minutes or until the mixture has frothed up. Combine the flour, salt and oil in a mixing bowl, add the yeast mixture and mix into a fairly soft dough which easily comes away from the sides of the bowl. Remove the dough from the bowl and knead on a floured surface for 5 minutes to form a smooth, elastic dough. (Alternatively, place flour, salt and oil into the bowl of a food processor and with the machine running, pour the yeast liquid through the feed tube, process until the mixture forms a ball around the knife and then for another 15 to 20 seconds to knead the dough.) Place the dough in a clean bowl and cover with a damp cloth; leave in a warm place for 45 minutes to 1 hour.

To make the pizza sauce

Heat the oil in a saucepan, add the tomatoes, tomato pureé, half the oregano, salt and pepper. Cook over a low heat, stirring occasionally for 15 minutes or until all the excess liquid has evaporated and you are left with a thick pureé. Cool. Preheat the oven to 475°F (240°C, gas mark 9).

Finally

Punch down the dough with your fists and knead lightly until smooth again. Grease the base of a pizza tray or flan ring. Roll the dough over the base, keeping the centre ⅛ in (2·5 mm) thick while making the edges 1 in (2·5 cm) thick. Spread the pizza sauce evenly over the pizza dough, but leaving the edges. Place the onions on top, followed by the mushroom, pepper, cheese and finally sprinkle with the remaining oregano. Bake the pizza in the preheated oven for 10 minutes or until the cheese is golden brown.

Recommended supplementary dish: Waldorf salad (see index for recipe).

Bombay Eggs　　　　*Serves 6 as a snack, 3 as a main meal*

Bombay eggs are rich in protein. Serve 1 per person with bread and pickles as a snack or 2 per person with the recommended supplementary dish as a main meal.

2 large onions, diced	1 teaspoon turmeric
8 oz (225 g) brown lentils	salt and black pepper to taste
2 tablespoons vegetable oil	6 hard boiled eggs, shelled
2 tablespoons grated Cheddar cheese	plain flour for dusting
2 tablespoons fresh coriander leaves *or* parsley, finely chopped	2 eggs, beaten wholemeal breadcrumbs for coating
1–2 teaspoons curry powder (depending on personal taste)	oil for deep frying

Put the onions and lentils in a large pan and mix well together. Cover them well with water, bring it to the boil and simmer for 1½ to 2 hours or until the lentils are very soft. Drain well, reserving the liquid for soup-making. Heat the oil in a frying pan, add the onions and lentils, stir continuously over a low heat, until all the moisture has evaporated and you are left with a fairly thick mixture. Add the cheese, coriander, curry powder (to taste), turmeric, salt and pepper, and mix well. Cool. Now divide the mixture into 6 equal portions and use each portion to coat one egg completely. Dust the coated eggs with seasoned flour, dip each into the beaten egg and then roll in breadcrumbs. Heat the oil for deep frying until it just starts to smoke. Deep fry the coated eggs three at a time to make the outside crisp and golden.

Recommended supplementary dish: Protein plus coleslaw or ginger and yoghurt rice salad (for recipes see index).

Courgettes Stuffed with Cottage Cheese   *Serves 4*

Serve on their own or with a tomato sauce (see index).

4 large courgettes
1 oz (25 g) butter
½ medium onion, finely chopped
1 clove garlic, crushed

8 oz (225 g) cottage cheese
8 oz (225 g) cooked long grain
  brown rice (4 oz/100 g raw rice)
salt and black pepper to taste

Wash and top and tail the courgettes, then slice them lengthwise down the middle. Place the courgettes in a saucepan and add enough water to cover. Bring to the boil and simmer for 5 to 7 minutes or until just tender. Drain and rinse the courgettes in cold water to prevent overcooking. Melt the butter in a large frying pan over medium heat, add the chopped onion and garlic and stir until the onion is soft and transparent. Scoop out the centre of the courgette halves with a teaspoon, leaving a thickness of ⅛ in (2·5 mm) all round. Finely chop the courgette flesh and add it to the onions and garlic in the pan. Cook, stirring occasionally, until all the moisture has evaporated, but do not brown. Let the mixture cool, stir in the cottage cheese and mix well. Add the cooked rice and season well with salt and pepper. Do not reheat. Place the courgette halves in a serving dish and pile the rice mixture down the centre of each courgette. Serve immediately.

Recommended supplementary dish: Mixed bean salad or lentil salad (for recipes see index).

Piperade   *Serves 3 as a main course, 4 as brunch*

A colourful dish from the Basque region of France. Be careful not to overcook the eggs. Serve with hot wholemeal toast.

2 tablespoons vegetable oil, preferably olive oil
1 lb (450 g) onions, finely sliced
1 large green pepper, cored, seeded and sliced
1 large red pepper, cored, seeded and sliced

1 lb (450 g) ripe tomatoes, chopped
salt and black pepper
6 eggs, beaten
fresh basil, chopped, *or* dried basil, crushed, to garnish

In a frying pan melt the oil over a medium heat. Add the onions and cook until soft but not coloured. Add the peppers and cook until soft. Stir in the tomatoes and season with salt and pepper. Cover and cook gently for 5 to 10 minutes or until thick. Pour in the eggs and stir continuously until the egg is lightly set (as you would for scrambled eggs). Sprinkle over with basil and serve immediately with hot wholemeal toast.

Recommended supplementary dish: Greek salad (for recipe see index).

Vegetarian Lasagne   *Serves 6*

This is a dish to serve to friends who think a meal without meat cannot be exciting.

1 small aubergine, roughly chopped
1 tablespoon vegetable oil
1 small onion, finely chopped
8 oz (225 g) mushrooms, sliced
8 oz (225 g) tinned tomatoes, coarsely chopped
2 tablespoons tomato purée
½ teaspoon dried basil
1 teaspoon dried oregano
pinch of brown sugar

salt and black pepper
12 oz (350 g) ricotta cheese
1 egg
8 oz (225 g) wholemeal lasagne, cooked and drained (for home-made lasagne see page 25)
6 oz (175 g) mozzarella cheese, grated
2 oz (50 g) Parmesan cheese

Place the chopped aubergine in a sieve or colander, sprinkle well with salt, cover and leave to drain for 30 minutes. Rinse well. Heat the oil in a saucepan, add the onion and cook over a moderate heat until soft. Add the aubergine and mushrooms and cook for a further 5 minutes. Add the tomatoes, tomato purée, basil, oregano and brown sugar, stir, cover and simmer for 30 minutes or until thick. Season with salt and black pepper.

Preheat the oven to 350°F (180°C, gas mark 4). In a bowl, combine the ricotta cheese and egg, and mix well. Spread a third of the aubergine sauce over the base of a baking dish, cover with half the lasagne, then spread the ricotta cheese mixture over. Continue layering with half the mozzarella cheese, a third of the aubergine sauce, the remaining lasagne, aubergine sauce, and mozzarella cheese. Sprinkle with Parmesan cheese. Bake in the preheated oven for 25 to 30 minutes, or until the cheese is golden. Serve immediately.

Recommended supplementary dishes: Basic mixed salad and one of the bean salads (for recipes see index).

Spinach and Yoghurt Crepes   *Serves 4 (3 pancakes each)*

Good on their own or with a sauce (for sauce recipes see index).

Pancake batter
4 oz (100 g) wholemeal flour
1 egg, beaten
10 fl oz (275 ml) milk
2 tablespoons vegetable oil

Filling
1 tablespoon vegetable margarine
1½ lb (700 g) fresh spinach, finely chopped
3 tablespoons fresh yoghurt
nutmeg
salt and pepper

To make the pancakes

Place the flour in a large mixing bowl, make a well in the centre of the flour and add the egg. Gradually whisk in half the milk and beat until smooth. Add the remaining milk and 1 tablespoon of oil.

Heat a 6-in (15-cm) omelette pan and wipe round the inside with a piece of absorbent paper dipped in a little of the remaining oil. Pour in enough batter to coat the base of the pan thinly. Cook until the underside is brown, turn over and cook for another 10 to 15 seconds. Turn out onto greaseproof paper. Repeat with the remaining batter, making 12 pancakes in all. Stack with greaseproof paper to prevent them sticking.

To make the filling

Melt the margarine in a saucepan over a low heat. Add the spinach and cook for 5 minutes, stirring occasionally. Remove from the heat and stir in the yoghurt, then season with nutmeg, salt and pepper.

Finally

Place a portion of the filling in the centre of each pancake, roll up like a cigar and place under a hot grill to warm through. Serve immediately.

Recommended supplementary dish: Potato, walnut and cottage cheese salad (for recipe see index).

Watercress and Onion Quiche   *Serves 4–6*

If watercress is unavailable, use 1 lb (450 g) fresh spinach instead.

Pastry
6 oz (175 g) wholemeal flour
2 oz (50 g) plain flour
pinch of salt
4 oz (100 g) vegetable margarine

Filling
1 tablespoon vegetable oil
1 small onion, finely chopped
6 bunches of watercress, washed,
    stalks removed
6 oz (175 g) cottage cheese
3 eggs beaten
2 oz (50 g) Parmesan cheese
5 fl oz (150 ml) milk
½ teaspoon freshly grated nutmeg
salt and pepper

To make the pastry

Place the flours and salt in a large mixing bowl and rub in the margarine until the mixture resembles breadcrumbs. Sprinkle 2 or 3 tablespoons iced water over the mixture and mix to a firm dough. On a lightly floured board roll out the pastry thinly and use it to line an 8-in (20-cm) flan ring. Chill for 30 minutes. Preheat the oven to 375°F (190°C, gas mark 5).

To prepare the filling

Heat the oil in a saucepan over medium heat, add the onion and cook until soft, but not coloured. Add the watercress and cook for a further 2 minutes or until the leaves are just soft. Cool slightly, add the cottage cheese, eggs, Parmesan and milk, and season with nutmeg, salt and pepper. Mix well.

Finally

Pour this mixture into the prepared flan case and bake in the preheated oven for 35 minutes, or until the centre of the flan is just firm and the top is golden. Can be served hot or cold.

Recommended supplementary dish: Red rice (see index for recipe) or mulligatawny soup with yoghurt (recipe below).

Mulligatawny Soup with Yoghurt   *Serves 4*

3 tablespoons vegetable oil
2 large onions, diced
1–2 teaspoons curry powder
1 clove garlic, crushed
1 lb (450 g) courgettes, diced
12 oz (350 g) tomatoes, diced
1 large potato, peeled and diced
16 fl oz (450 ml) vegetable stock *or*
  water

salt and black pepper to taste
4 oz (100 g) cooked brown rice,
  drained
2 fl oz (50 ml) natural low fat
  yoghurt
1 tablespoon chopped parsley (to
  garnish)

Melt the oil in a saucepan, add the onion and cook until soft but not browned. Add the curry powder (to taste) and cook stirring continuously for 2 to 3 minutes. Add the garlic, courgettes, tomatoes, potato and stock. Bring to the boil, and simmer for 30 minutes or until all the vegetables are soft. Cool slightly, then liquidize to a purée. Return to the saucepan, and season with salt and black pepper. Stir in the cooked rice and swirl the yoghurt on top. Sprinkle the parsley over the dish and serve immediately.

Watercress, Leek and Noodle Bake in Cheese   *Serves 4–6*

2 tablespoons vegetable oil
1 large onion, finely chopped
2 bunches watercress, washed,
  stalks removed
1½ lb (700 g) leeks, washed, sliced
  thinly
salt and black pepper
2 eggs, lightly beaten
12 oz (350 g) wholewheat tagliatelle
  or noodles, cooked

2 oz (50 g) Parmesan cheese
4 oz (100 g) wholewheat
  breadcrumbs

Sauce
2 oz (50 g) butter
2 oz (50 g) wholemeal flour
16 fl oz (450 ml) milk

To prepare the bake

Heat the oil in a saucepan, add the onion, watercress and leeks. Cook gently for 10 to 15 minutes, stirring occasionally until tender. Season with salt and pepper. Stir in the eggs, mixing well. Arrange half the cooked tagliatelle in a baking dish. Sprinkle half the Parmesan cheese over this and cover it with half the leek and watercress mixture. Add layers of the remaining tagliatelle, Parmesan and watercress and leek mixture. Preheat the oven to 400°F (200°C, gas mark 6).

To make the sauce

Melt the butter in a saucepan, add the flour and cook for one minute. Gradually add the milk, bring to the boil, stirring continuously until thick and smooth. Season with salt and pepper and pour over the top of the watercress and leeks.

Finally

Sprinkle the breadcrumbs over the dish and bake in the preheated oven for 20 to 25 minutes or until golden. Serve straight from the baking dish.

Recommended supplementary dishes: Basic mixed salad and a bean salad (for recipes see index), or mulligatawny soup (recipe above).

Nut Kromeskies   *Serves 4*

A 'kromeski' is another name for a croquette. Serve kromeskies with a cheese sauce (see index).

1 oz (25 g) Brazil nuts	1 tablespoon finely chopped parsley
2 oz (50 g) walnut pieces	1 teaspoon caraway seeds
3 oz (75 g) hazelnuts	pinch of ground nutmeg
1 medium onion, finely chopped	salt and pepper to taste
3 oz (75 g) carrots, peeled and grated	2 eggs, beaten
	wholemeal flour for coating
4 oz (100 g) fresh wholemeal breadcrumbs	2 oz (50 g) natural bran
	vegetable oil for deep frying

Put all the nuts on a baking sheet and lightly brown them under a moderate grill. Remove any skins from the nuts by rubbing them between the ends of a dry cloth. Chop the nuts finely and mix them with the onion, carrots, breadcrumbs, parsley, caraway seeds, nutmeg, salt and pepper. Stir in half the beaten egg and stir well. Divide the mixture into 8 equal portions and shape each into a round. Coat each kromeski in flour, followed by beaten egg and then natural bran. Heat the oil and deep fry the nut kromeskies for 5 to 8 minutes or until golden brown.

Recommended supplementary dishes: Brown rice plus apple and celery salad with curry dressing (for recipes see index).

Nut Roast with Tomato and Basil Sauce   *Serves 4–6*

This nut roast is excellent served with the special tomato sauce given in the recipe below. Make the sauce while the nut roast is cooking. If fresh basil in unavailable, make the tomato sauce given on page 112.

1 oz (25 g) butter
4 oz (100 g) onion, finely chopped
2 oz (50 g) Brazil nuts, finely chopped
2 oz (50 g) hazelnuts, finely chopped
4 oz (100 g) unsalted peanuts
4 oz (100 g) fresh brown breadcrumbs
2 eggs, beaten
4 oz (100 g) grated Cheddar cheese
salt and pepper

Sauce
8 large ripe tomatoes, skinned
1 small onion, finely chopped
½ oz (15 g) butter
pinch of sugar
5 basil stalks
salt and pepper
10 basil leaves, finely chopped

To prepare the nut roast

Preheat the oven to 350°F (180°C, gas mark 4). Melt the butter in a large saucepan and sauté the onion in it until golden brown. Mix in the nuts, breadcrumbs, egg and cheese and season well with salt and pepper. Grease a 1½-lb (700-g) loaf tin. Press the nut mixture evenly into the tin. Bake in the preheated oven for about 45 minutes or until golden brown.

To prepare the sauce

Cut the tomatoes into quarters and remove the seeds. Chop the flesh roughly. Sauté the onion in the butter until soft and transparent. Add the chopped tomato, the pinch of sugar and the basil stalks. Cook over a low heat until most of the liquid has evaporated. Remove from the heat. Remove basil stalks, season with salt and pepper and add the chopped basil leaves and heat through.

Finally

Cool the nut roast for a few minutes before turning it out of the tin. Pour the tomato sauce over the roast and serve.

Recommended supplementary dish: Ginger and yoghurt rice salad (for recipe see index).

Dishes containing grains

Stuffed Green Peppers   *Serves 4*

Two fillings are given. The protein in the first comes from a combination of hazelnuts and brown rice and in the second from mixed nuts and cheese. Serve the stuffed peppers with or without a sauce (for sauces see index) and the recommended supplementary dish given below.

4 large red or green peppers
1 tablespoon vegetable oil

Preheat oven to 400°F (200°C, gas mark 6). Cut the tops off the peppers, remove the cores and seeds. Choose one of the following fillings.

Filling 1: Hazelnut, Rice and Orange

2 tablespoons vegetable oil
1 medium onion, diced
2 stalks celery, finely chopped
4 oz (100 g) coarsely chopped
  hazelnuts
12 oz (350 g) cooked long grain
  brown rice

1 medium size orange, peeled and
  chopped small
2 oz (50 g) raisins, plumped in a
  little boiling water, drained
1 egg, beaten
1 teaspoon cinnamon
salt to taste

Heat the oil in a frying pan and sauté the onion, celery and hazel nuts until the onion is lightly coloured. Combine this mixture with the remaining ingredients.

Filling 2: Cheese and Nut

6 oz (175 g) Cheddar cheese, grated
6 oz (175 g) ground mixed nuts (*or*
  a single ground nut of your
  choice)
1 large onion, finely diced
3 stalks celery, finely chopped
½ teaspoon crushed dried thyme (*or*
  1 teaspoon fresh thyme if
  available)

½ teaspoon crushed dried basil (*or* 1
  teaspoon chopped fresh basil if
  available)
1 large egg, beaten
salt and black pepper to taste

Combine all the ingredients and mix well together.

Pack the filling into the peppers. Brush the peppers all over with oil and put them in a baking dish. Put the tops back on the peppers and bake them for 35 minutes.

Variations:

1. The same fillings can be used to stuff other vegetables, e.g. aubergines, courgettes, potatoes, vine leaves.
2. Increase the protein content of the fillings by adding 4 oz (100 g) cooked beans to them.

Recommended supplementary dish: Serve peppers stuffed with the hazelnut, rice and orange filling with Greek salad; and peppers stuffed with cheese and nut filling with plain bulgar wheat or brown rice and a basic mixed salad (for recipes see index).

Brown Rice Croquettes   *Serves 4*

This is a good recipe for using up leftover cooked vegetables and/or cooked rice.

1 lb (450 g) short *or* long grain
   cooked brown rice, drained
either 2 medium onions, finely
   diced, 2 medium carrots, finely
   diced *or* 1 lb (450 g) mixed
   cooked vegetables
4 oz (100 g) wholemeal flour
salt and black pepper to taste
2 eggs, beaten

wholemeal breadcrumbs *or* flour for
   coating
oil for frying

Garnishing
Parmesan cheese or grated Cheddar
   cheese
parsley, chopped

Combine the rice with the onions and carrots or cooked vegetables, the flour, seasoning and beaten eggs and mix well. Wet your hands in cold water and form the mixture into 8 croquettes. Keeping your hands wet stops the mixture sticking to them. Roll the croquettes in breadcrumbs or flour. Now shallow fry them for about 5 minutes on both sides over a low heat or until nicely browned. Alternatively, deep fry them in hot oil for 3 to 4 minutes. Serve sprinkled with cheese and parsley.

Recommended supplementary dish: Mexican red bean salad (for recipe see index).

Nut and Vegetable Brown Rice Casserole   *Serves 4*

A simple but wholesome dish and easy to make. Try it also using different vegetables than given here or with the addition of herbs and spices to your own taste.

2 tablespoons vegetable oil
1 medium onion, diced
1 small carrot, grated
4 oz (100 g) Chinese cabbage *or* spinach, shredded
2 oz (50 g) bean sprouts

4 oz (100 g) walnuts, chopped
½ teaspoon hot pepper sauce
soy sauce to taste
1 lb (450 g) cooked long grain brown rice
2 eggs, beaten

Preheat the oven to 350°F (180°C, gas mark 4). Heat the oil in a large, heavy pan then add the onions and sauté them until soft, stir in the carrot and cook over a moderate heat a further 2 minutes. Add the cabbage or spinach, mix well, cover the pan and cook until the greens are wilted. Stir in the bean sprouts, walnuts, hot pepper sauce, soy sauce and cooked rice, mix well and then stir in the beaten egg. Turn the contents of the pan into a lightly greased casserole, cover and bake for 25 to 30 minutes. Serve.

Variation:

Add 4 oz (100 g) cooked beans to the rice mixture before baking.

Recommended supplementary dish: Chickpea and Cheddar cheese salad (see index for recipe).

Spinach Parcels   *Serves 4*

If spinach is not available, or for variation, vine leaves or cabbage leaves (lightly blanched in boiling water) may be used instead.

16 large, unblemished spinach leaves, washed, stalks removed
salt and pepper
1 tablespoon vegetable oil
1 large onion, finely chopped
1 clove garlic, finely chopped
2 oz (50 g) pine nuts
10 oz (275 g) mushrooms, washed and coarsely chopped

6 oz (175 g) cooked long grain brown rice (3 oz/75 g raw rice)
1 tablespoon fresh parsley, chopped
1 large egg, lightly beaten
freshly grated nutmeg
vegetable margarine for greasing
4 large ripe tomatoes, cut into thick slices
2 fl oz (50 ml) water

Bring a saucepan of salted water to the boil, add the spinach leaves 2 or 3 at a time and blanch them until just limp. Remove them with a slotted spoon and immediately plunge the leaves into iced water to cool. Remove the leaves and lay them flat on absorbent paper to dry. Continue until all the leaves are done. Heat the oil in a saucepan, add the onion, garlic and pine nuts and cook until golden. Add the mushrooms and cook for a further 5 minutes until tender. Cool, then add the cooked rice, parsley and egg, season with nutmeg and salt and pepper and mix well.

Place a portion of stuffing in the centre of each spinach leaf. Fold in both the sides and roll up carefully. Lightly grease a shallow baking dish and place a layer of tomato slices on the bottom. Tightly pack in the spinach parcels in one layer and pour the water over them. Bring the water to the boil, reduce the heat, cover with a lid and simmer very gently for 30 minutes. Serve immediately from the baking dish.

Recommended supplementary dish: Bulgar wheat gratin or tabbouleh (for recipes see index).

Rice with Spinach and Yoghurt   *Serves 4–6*

3 tablespoons vegetable oil
1 medium onion, chopped
1 lb (450 g) spinach, washed, chopped *or* 8 oz (225 g) frozen spinach, defrosted, drained, chopped
6 fl oz (175 ml) natural low fat yoghurt

1 teaspoon cinnamon
salt and black pepper to taste
1 lb (450 g) cooked long grain brown rice
1 egg, beaten
4 oz (100 g) Cheddar cheese, grated *or* thin slices of mozzarella

Preheat the oven to 350°F (180°C, gas mark 4). Heat the oil in a large pan and sauté the onion until softened. Add the spinach and sauté until wilted, and softened. Remove the pan from the heat and stir in the yoghurt, cinnamon and salt and black pepper. Combine one-third of the rice with the beaten egg and put this mixture into the bottom of a lightly greased casserole dish (about 9 in/23 cm across). Now make alternate layers of the spinach/yoghurt mixture and remaining rice, ending up with a layer of rice. Top with cheese and cover. Bake in the preheated oven for 30 minutes. Remove the cover from the casserole about 10 minutes before the end of the cooking time.

Recommended supplementary dish: Lentil salad (for recipe see index).

Nut and Fruit Rice   *Serves 4*

This exotic dish of Middle Eastern origin is in fact easy to prepare and economical. With a combination of rice, milk and nuts it is protein-rich but the liberal use of butter gives it a high fat content. If you wish you could replace the butter with an unsaturated seed or nut oil such as sesame or peanut. Another variation is to turn the dish into a nutritious dessert or invalid food by replacing the salt with 2 tablespoons honey or brown sugar.

1 lb (450 g) cooked brown rice
4 fl oz (100 ml) milk
8 oz (225 g) mixed dates and raisins
4 oz (100 g) blanched almonds *or*
  walnuts, chopped

grated peel of 1 orange
1 teaspoon salt
3 tablespoons butter, melted

Preheat the oven to 325°F (170°C, gas mark 3). Place one-third of the rice in the bottom of a heavy casserole and pour on the milk. Sprinkle half the fruit, nuts, orange peel and salt over the top. Cover with half the remaining rice and layer again with the remaining fruit, nuts, orange peel and salt. Top with the last of the rice and pour the melted butter evenly over. Cover the casserole and place it in a shallow dish containing 1 in (2.5 cm) water. Place the dish in the oven and bake for 50 minutes to 1 hour.

Recommended supplementary dish: Basic mixed salad and/or apple and celery salad with curry dressing (for recipes see index).

Cauliflower and Potato Pilau   *Serves 4*

Pilau is the Indian equivalent of the Arab pilaf or the Spanish paella. It is essentially a dish of rice cooked with other ingredients in the same pot. This recipe and the two that follow may be used as a basis for your own improvisations using different vegetables, nuts and spices.

3 tablespoons vegetable oil
2 medium potatoes, peeled, diced
½ small head cauliflower, in sprigs
1 medium onion, finely sliced
2 cloves garlic, crushed
12 oz (350 g) long grain brown rice
6 oz (175 g) unroasted peanuts
½ teaspoon ground cloves
½ teaspoon ground turmeric
½ teaspoon ground ginger

1 teaspoon cumin seeds
½ teaspoon garam masala *or*
  curry powder
1 teaspoon cinnamon
1½ pt (850 ml) water, boiling
salt to taste

Garnishing
slices of hard boiled egg
roasted almonds

Heat the oil in a heavy pan, add the potatoes and fry until they are half-cooked, remove them from the pan and set aside. Add the cauliflower sprigs and fry until they are half-cooked. Remove them from the pan and set aside. Add the onions and garlic and sauté until golden brown. Put in the rice and peanuts and fry, stirring, for 2 to 3 minutes. Sprinkle in the spices, mix well and stir fry for another few minutes. Pour in the water, stir and season to taste with salt. Cook, uncovered, over a moderate heat until half the water in the pot has been absorbed or has evaporated. Add the part-cooked potatoes and cauliflower. Now tightly cover the pot. Reduce the heat and leave the pot to simmer until the rice is tender and fluffy (30 to 40 minutes). Serve garnished with slices of hard boiled eggs and a sprinkling of roasted almonds.

Recommended supplementary dishes: Wholemeal chapattis, chickpeas in yoghurt and French dressing (for recipes see index).

Spicy Cashew and Almond Pilau   *Serves 4*

3 tablespoons vegetable oil
1-in (2·5-cm) stick cinnamon
3 cloves
3 cardomom seeds
6 pepper corns
½ teaspoon cumin seeds

12 oz (350 g) long grain brown rice
1½ pt (850 ml) water, boiling
2 oz (50 g) almonds, blanched
2 oz (50 g) cashews, lightly roasted
2 oz (50 g) sultanas
salt to taste

Heat the oil in a heavy pan and fry the cinnamon, cloves, cardomoms, pepper corns and cumin seeds for 2 to 3 minutes. Add the rice and stir fry for 5 minutes. Pour in the water, reduce the heat, cover and simmer until the rice is nearly tender. Now stir in the nuts and sultanas and salt to taste. Recover the pot and cook until the rice is tender.

Recommended supplementary dish: Wholemeal chapattis, natural low fat yoghurt, crisp green salad.

Rice and Lentil Pilau   *Serves 4*

3 tablespoons vegetable oil
1 medium onion, chopped
8 oz (225 g) long grain brown rice
1 pt (575 ml) water *or* vegetable
  stock
8 oz (225 g) brown lentils, soaked
  3–4 hours, drained

1 tablespoon tomato purée
½ teaspoon cumin seeds
½ teaspoon coriander seeds, crushed
½ teaspoon cinnamon
4 oz (100 g) raisins
4 oz (100 g) sunflower seeds
salt to taste

Heat the oil in a heavy pan and sauté the onion until softened. Stir in the rice and cook, stirring, for 3 to 4 minutes. Add the remaining ingredients and mix well. Bring to the boil, cover the pot, reduce the heat and simmer for 50 minutes to 1 hour or until the rice is tender and the lentils are cooked.

Recommended supplementary dishes: Wholemeal chapattis and chickpeas in yoghurt.

Vegetable Paella   *Serves 4*

Paella is a famous Spanish dish named after the large flat pan with two handles in which it is cooked. The pan doubles as a serving dish. A large frying pan and a serving dish do the job just as well, although a little of the drama of bringing the food straight from the stove to the table is lost. Normally paella is cooked with meat and fish; here we provide the protein content with nuts and cheese.

3 tablespoons vegetable oil
2 cloves garlic, crushed
2 medium onions, sliced
2 medium green peppers, cored, seeded, sliced
2 medium tomatoes, chopped
12 oz (375 g) long grain brown rice
1½ pt (850 ml) water *or* vegetable stock

salt and black pepper to taste
4 oz (100 g) cucumber, peeled and diced
2 sticks celery, chopped
4 oz (100 g) chopped nuts
2 oz (50 g) olives (optional)
6 oz (175 g) Cheddar cheese, grated

Heat the oil in a heavy frying pan and sauté the garlic and onions until they start to colour. Add the pepper and sauté for a further 2 to 3 minutes. Stir in the tomatoes and rice and cook over a low heat, stirring, for 5 minutes. Pour in the water or stock, season to taste with salt and black pepper and boil rapidly for 5 minutes. Add the cucumber, celery and chopped nuts, reduce the heat to a simmer and cook until the rice is tender and all the liquid is absorbed. Add more water if the rice dries up before it is tender. Serve garnished with olives and cheese.

Recommended supplementary dishes: Wholemeal French bread and basic mixed salad (for recipes see index).

Lasagne Covent Garden   *Serves 4*

This dish is a nutritious mixture containing an excellent balance of proteins, vitamins, minerals and carbohydrates and a low fat content.

12 oz (350 g) carrots, peeled and
sliced
12 oz (350 g) parsnips, peeled and
sliced
½ oz (15 g) vegetable margarine
salt and freshly ground black
pepper to taste
6 sheets wholemeal lasagne
(see page 25 for recipe)
12 oz (350 g) cottage cheese
2 oz (50 g) walnuts, roughly
chopped

2 lb (900 g) fresh spinach, cooked
soft in a little water *or* 1 lb (450 g)
frozen spinach, thawed, drained
well, chopped
¼ teaspoon nutmeg
4 oz (100 g) mozzarella cheese,
sliced thinly

Garnishing
1 large tomato, sliced thinly
fresh or dried basil

Preheat the oven to 350°F (180°C, gas mark 4). Cook the carrots in a large saucepan, containing enough boiling salted water to cover, for 5 minutes, then add the parsnips and continue cooking for a further 10 minutes or until both vegetables are very tender. Drain the vegetables well and mash together with the butter, season with salt and pepper. Spread the mixture onto the base of an ovenproof dish. Cover it with three sheets of the lasagne (uncooked), then with the cottage cheese mixed with the chopped walnuts. Cover this layer with the remaining lasagne. Spread over this the spinach seasoned with nutmeg, salt and pepper. Place the cheese slices over the top and bake in the preheated oven for 30 minutes or until the lasagne is tender and the cheese golden brown. Remove from the oven and decorate with slices of tomato and fresh basil.

Recommended supplementary dishes: Wholemeal bread and basic mixed salad (for recipes see index).

Lasagne with Wholemeal Breadcrumbs and Cheese   *Serves 4*

Not only a useful way of using up leftover stale bread, this is a quick and unusual lasagne recipe.

4 fl oz (100 ml) olive oil *or* sesame seed oil
1 lb (450 g) wholemeal lasagne (see page 25 for recipe)
4 oz (100 g) wholemeal breadcrumbs, lightly toasted

freshly milled black pepper
1 tablespoon finely chopped parsley
4 oz (100 g) Parmesan *or* Cheddar cheese, grated

Bring a large pan of salted water to the boil and add 1 teaspoon of the oil to it, then the lasagne. Meanwhile season the breadcrumbs with salt and black pepper. Cook the lasagne until tender. Drain and place it in a serving dish. Heat the oil in a small pan and drop in the breadcrumbs. Immediately remove the pan from the heat. Pour the oil and breadcrumbs over the lasagne, sprinkle parsley and cheese over the dish and serve.

Recommended supplementary dish: Red bean, tomato and onion salad (for recipe see index).

Macaroni Salad   *Serves 4*

This is a substantial salad and nutritious enough to serve as the major part of a cold main meal.

8 oz (225 g) wholemeal macaroni
salt
6 tablespoons olive, sesame *or* sunflower oil
4 oz (100 g) blanched almonds
4 oz (100 g) mushrooms, sliced
½ small onion, diced
2 sticks celery, chopped

4 oz (100 g) cheese, grated
juice of 1 lemon
pinch cayenne
2 eggs, hard boiled, shelled and sliced
1 oz (25 g) sunflower seeds, lightly dry roasted

Bring a large pan of salted water to the boil and cook the pasta *al dente*. Drain the pasta immediately and rinse under cold water. Put the cool pasta in a serving bowl and stir in 1 tablespoon oil. Fry the almonds in 1 tablespoon of oil until just browned, add the mushrooms and fry, stirring, until softened. Remove the pan from the heat and stir the contents into the macaroni. Add the remaining oil and the other ingredients to the pasta, salt to taste and mix well. Serve.

Recomended supplementary dish: Greek salad (for recipe see index).

Lentils with Bulgar Wheat and Yoghurt   *Serves 4*

This dish of Lebanese origin is prepared from an unusual combination
of ingredients. It is nevertheless simple and quick to prepare and the
bulgar wheat, lentils and yoghurt combination provides a good
protein mixture.

8 oz (225 g) brown *or* green lentils,
washed, picked over, soaked 4
hours or more, drained
1½ pt (850 ml) water *plus* 8 fl oz
(225 ml) water
2 medium onions, diced

4 fl oz (100 ml) vegetable oil (olive
oil is recommended)
8 oz (225 g) bulgar wheat
salt and pepper to taste
6 fl oz (175 ml) natural low fat
yoghurt

Bring the lentils to the boil in 1½ pt (850 ml) water in a heavy pan.
Meanwhile fry the onions in the oil until golden brown. Drain the oil
into the boiling lentils and water, reduce the heat and gently simmer
the lentils. Pour 8 fl oz (225 ml) of water over the fried onions and
simmer them over a low heat for 10 minutes. Pour the onions and
water into the lentil pot and continue cooking for another 10 minutes.
Now add the bulgar to the pot and return to the boil. Reduce the heat,
cover and simmer for 25 to 30 minutes or until all the water is
absorbed. Season to taste with salt and pepper and serve hot, topped
with natural yoghurt.

Recommended supplementary dishes: Wholemeal pitta bread and basic
mixed salad (for recipes see index).

Baked Vegetable and Wholewheat Loaf   *Serves 4*

The recommended supplementary dish for this recipe is leek and
tomato bake (see recipe below). It can be baked at the same time as the
wholewheat loaf.

8 oz (225 g) wholewheat berries
1 large onion, sliced
8 oz (225 g) potatoes, peeled and
cubed
4 oz (100 g) mushrooms, sliced
(optional)
8 oz (225 g) carrots, finely chopped
2 medium green peppers, cored,
seeded and chopped

1 tablespoon tomato purée
4 oz (100 g) wholemeal flour *or*
brown breadcrumbs
4 tablespoons vegetable oil
1 teaspoon dried thyme
salt and black pepper to taste
4 oz (100 g) cheese, grated

Boil the wholewheat in plenty of water for 15 minutes. Drain. Preheat the oven to 375°F (190°C, gas mark 5). Combine partially cooked wheat with the remaining ingredients, except the cheese, mix well and season to taste. Place the mixture in a deep baking dish or bread tin, sprinkle cheese on top and bake for 50 to 60 minutes or until a knife pushed into the centre of the bake comes out clean. Remove the tin from the oven and allow to cool a little. Run a knife around the edge of the loaf and then tip it out carefully onto a serving dish. Serve on its own or with a béchamel sauce (see index).

Recommended supplementary dish: Leek and tomato bake (recipe below).

Leek and Tomato Bake   *Serves 4*

4 oz (100 g) vegetable margarine	salt and black pepper
2 large leeks, sliced thinly into rings	4 oz (100 g) wholemeal
4 large tomatoes, sliced thinly	breadcrumbs
3 tablespoons finely chopped	
coriander *or* basil *or* 3 teaspoons	
dried basil	

Preheat the oven to 375°F (190°C, gas mark 5). Melt half the margarine in a frying pan. Add the leeks and fry until soft but not brown. Remove them from the heat and spread half the leeks into a greased baking dish. Cover with half the tomato slices and sprinkle with half the fresh or dried herbs. Season with salt and black pepper. Make another layer of leek rings and tomato slices and sprinkle with the remaining herbs. Season with salt and black pepper. Cover with breadcrumbs and dot the remaining margarine over the top. Bake in the preheated oven for 30 minutes. Serve hot.

Chinese–Style Wholewheat   *Serves 4*

Once the wheat berries are cooked this is a very quick dish to prepare. It is the wholewheat version of Chinese fried rice.

2 eggs	1 lb (450 g) cooked wholewheat,
1 tablespoon butter	cold (for cooking instructions see
4 tablespoons vegetable oil	page 21)
1 medium onion, finely chopped	4 oz (100 g) mushrooms, diced
3 sticks celery, diced	4 teaspoons soy sauce
2 green *or* red peppers, cored,	salt and black pepper to taste
seeded, diced	

Beat the eggs together, heat the butter in a large frying pan, and prepare two thin omelettes. Cut the omelettes into thin strips and set aside. Heat the oil in the frying pan. When it is hot, add the onion, celery and peppers and sauté until nearly tender. Now add the wholewheat and mushrooms and cook, stirring constantly, for a further 5 minutes. Just before serving mix in the egg strips, soy sauce, salt and black pepper. Serve immediately.

Recommended supplementary dish: Bean and beansprout salad (for recipe see index).

V's Savoury Oat Slices   *Serves 4*

Serve on their own or with parsley sauce (see index).

2 oz (50 g) vegetable margarine
1 medium onion, finely chopped
4 oz (100 g) mushrooms, chopped
5 oz (150 g) rolled oats
6 oz (175 g) carrot, finely grated
5 oz (150 g) cheese, grated

1 egg, beaten
1 clove garlic, crushed
1 tablespoon soy sauce
1 tablespoon tomato purée
1 teaspoon dried basil
salt and black pepper to taste

Preheat the oven to 325°F (170°C, gas mark 3). Melt the margarine in a pan and gently cook the onion and mushrooms for 5 minutes. Transfer them to a mixing bowl and add all the other ingredients. Season to taste with salt and pepper and mix well. Press the mixture into a greased square baking dish and bake for 25 to 30 minutes. Remove from the hot oven and allow to cool a little before cutting into squares. Serve hot or cold.

Recommended supplementary dishes: Baked or boiled corn on the cob and a bean salad (for recipes see index).

Aubergine Samosas   *Serves 4 as a main meal, 8 as an appetiser*

Small half-moon-shaped packets of dough stuffed with a tasty aubergine filling and then deep fried. On their own these samosas are not very high in protein, but served topped with grated cheese, rice, cucumber slices in yoghurt and a green salad, they form the centrepiece of a nutritious and flavoursome meal.

Dough
8 oz (225 g) wholewheat flour
½ teaspoon salt
4 tablespoons vegetable oil
6–8 fl oz (175–225 ml) water
oil for frying

Filling
1 large aubergine *or* 2 small ones
  weighing approx 1 lb (450 g)
salt to taste
1 tablespoon vegetable oil
2 cloves garlic
½ teaspoon ground allspice
2 tablespoons tomato purée

To make the dough

Combine the flour and salt in a bowl, stir in 3 tablespoons oil and mix well. Add the water a little at a time until you have a firm dough. Knead well for about 10 minutes, until smooth. (If you have a food processor, put the flour, salt and oil into the bowl and with the machine running pour the water in a slow stream through the feed tube, adding just enough to enable the dough to form a ball around the knife. Stop adding liquid and allow the dough to make 10 more turns around the bowl before turning the processor off.) Brush the dough with the remaining oil and cover with a cloth until ready for use.

To make the filling

Finely chop the aubergine, place the pieces in a sieve or colander and sprinkle them with salt. Leave for 1 hour. Rinse well and pat dry with kitchen paper. Sauté the aubergine in the oil with the garlic and allspice until soft. Stir in the tomato purée, season with pepper and cool.

Finally

Divide the dough into 16 equal parts and roll each into a ball. Roll out each ball on a well-floured surface to form a 4-in (10-cm) round. Spoon a portion of the filling onto each round. Dampen half the circumference of each round and fold the other half over to form half-moon shapes. Press the edges to seal them. Pour 3 or 4 in (7 or 10 cm) oil into a deep pan and heat to about 350°F (180°C). Deep fry the samosas a few at a time for 2 to 3 minutes or until golden brown. Remove them from the oil and drain them well on kitchen paper. Serve immediately.

Recommended supplementary dishes: As suggested in the introduction to the recipe, or rice, ginger and yoghurt salad (for recipe see index).

Indonesian Rice Salad   *Serves 4*

I recently wrote a book on Indonesian cookery and during my research I came across the basis of this recipe. It is not authentic Indonesian but it's a good rice salad.

Salad
1 lb (450 g) cooked long grain
  brown rice, cooled
1 medium green pepper, cored,
  seeded, chopped
1 small onion, finely diced
4 oz (100 g) bean sprouts
4 oz (100 g) tinned water chestnuts,
  sliced (optional)
1 oz (25 g) sesame seeds, lightly dry
  roasted
2 oz (50 g) cashew nuts, lightly dry
  roasted
2 tablespoons finely chopped
  parsley

Dressing
4 fl oz (100 ml) fresh orange juice
2 fl oz (50 ml) olive, sunflower *or*
  other vegetable oil
3 tablespoons soy sauce (Japanese
  variety recommended)
juice of 1 lemon
1 clove garlic, crushed
1-in (2·5-cm) piece fresh ginger
  root, peeled, grated (optional)
salt and black pepper to taste

Garnishing
pineapple chunks
desiccated coconut, lightly dry
  roasted

Combine the salad ingredients and mix well. Combine the dressing ingredients and mix well. Toss the salad in the dressing and garnish the top with pineapple chunks and coconut.

Recommended supplementary dishes: Wholemeal bread and a bean or lentil salad (for receipes see index).

Vegetable Couscous   *Serves 6–8*

This recipe is from my book *Middle Eastern Vegetarian Cookery* (Rider and Company, 1982). Couscous is a wheat grain product made from semolina, and it is also the name of the famous dish of which couscous is the main ingredient. Until recent times couscous grain was always made by hand, a tricky job requiring skill and experience, but nowadays, fortunately, it is available prepared and only needs cooking. The couscous is steamed over a rich sauce or stew and then served in a mountainous heap with the sauce poured over. It is never cooked in the sauce. A special pot called a couscousier is traditionally used for cooking the sauce and simultaneously steaming the couscous, but a saucepan with a snug-fitting colander on top will do just as well.

  Couscous, with its combination of grains, beans and vegetables, provides an exciting and nutritious meal. Incidentally, the vegetable combination can be changed to suit whatever is in season. I have not suggested a supplementary dish since this couscous is a complete meal in itself.

2 oz (50 g) butter *or* vegetable oil
3 cloves garlic, crushed
2 medium onions, quartered
6 small courgettes, cut in 1-in (2·5-cm) pieces
2 medium green peppers, seeded, cored and cut into thick strips
2 large potatoes, scrubbed or peeled, and coarsely chopped
4 medium carrots, peeled, cut in half crosswise, then sliced lengthwise
2 small turnips, cut in half then sliced lengthwise
2 pt (1·1 litres) water
1 lb (450 g) couscous
8 oz (225 g) chickpeas, cooked and drained

1 lb (450 g) fresh tomatoes, quartered *or* 1 lb (100 g) tinned tomatoes
4 oz (100 g) sultanas, apricots *or* raisins, soaked and drained
1½ teaspoons ground coriander
1½ teaspoons ground cumin
2 teaspoons turmeric
1½ teaspoons cayenne
1–2 small chilli peppers, seeded, chopped
salt and black pepper to taste

Garnishing
2 eggs, hard boiled, shelled, sliced

In a heavy saucepan or in the bottom of a couscousier melt the butter, add the next seven ingredients in the above list and sauté, stirring, over a moderate heat for 5 minutes. Add half the water and bring to the boil. Reduce the heat and set to simmer. Meanwhile place the couscous in a large bowl and gently stir in 1 pt (575 ml) cold water. Drain immediately and allow the wet grains to stand for 10 minutes. As they swell up, rake them with your fingers to prevent lumps forming. Turn the grains into the top of a couscousier or into a colander and place it over the cooking vegetables. Leave to steam gently for 20 minutes. Remove the top of the couscousier or the colander and add to the cooking vegetables the remaining ingredients and remaining water. Return the vegetables to the boil and then reduce the heat and simmer for 15 minutes. Stir the couscous grains to break up any lumps that have formed and put the couscous back over the cooking vegetables. Cook and steam for a final 15 minutes. Pile the grains on a large serving dish. Drain off some of the liquid from the vegetables into a separate bowl. Pour the vegetables over the couscous and serve with the cooking liquid and a hot pepper sauce or harissa in separate bowls. Finally garnish with slices of hard boiled egg.

Dishes containing pulses

Lentil Curry   *Serves 4*

2 tablespoons vegetable oil
8 oz (225 g) brown *or* green lentils,
   washed and drained
2 medium onions, thinly sliced
2 medium green peppers, cored,
   seeded and chopped

2 cloves garlic, crushed
2 teaspoons curry powder
½ teaspoon dry English mustard
1 tablespoon tomato purée
16 fl oz (450 ml) water
salt to taste

Heat the oil in a large pot and add the lentils. Stir them for 2 to 3 minutes and then add the onion, green pepper, garlic, curry powder and mustard. Sauté, stirring, until the onion is soft and transparent. Add the tomato purée, water and salt and bring the mixture to the boil. Cover the pan, reduce the heat and simmer until the lentils are tender (about 35 to 40 minutes). Towards the end of the cooking time taste the curry and add more curry powder if you wish. Add more water if the curry is too dry, or leave the lid off the pan if it is too thin.

Recommended supplementary dishes: Low fat natural yoghurt, wholewheat chapattis and a green salad.

Winter Lentil Stew   *Serves 4*

2 tablespoons vegetable oil
1 medium onion, sliced
2 sticks celery, chopped
4 oz (100 g) brown *or* green lentils,
   washed and drained
16 fl oz (450 ml) water

8 oz (225 g) tinned tomatoes
2 medium potatoes, peeled and
   diced
½ teaspoon dried rosemary
salt and black pepper to taste
4 oz (100 g) Cheddar cheese

Heat the oil in a saucepan and add the onion and celery. Sauté until the onion is softened and golden and then stir in the lentils. Pour in the water and tomatoes and mix well. Add the potatoes and rosemary and season to taste with salt and black pepper. Bring to the boil, cover, reduce heat and simmer until the lentils and potatoes are tender (approximately 35 to 40 minutes). Serve garnished with grated cheese.

Recommended supplementary dishes: A cooked grain such as brown rice, wholewheat or kasha and a green salad.

Lentils with Wholemeal Noodles   *Serves 4*

A nutritious, filling and tasty way of combining complementary protein foods.

2 tablespoons vegetable oil
1 large onion, diced
2 cloves garlic, crushed
½ teaspoon ground cumin
½ teaspoon ground coriander
16 oz (450 g) cooked whole lentils, drained

salt and black pepper to taste
8 oz (225 g) wholewheat noodles *or* spaghetti, cooked, drained (see page 25 for home-made noodle recipe)
4 oz (100 g) Cheddar cheese, grated

Put the oil in a large saucepan and add the onion and garlic. Sauté until golden. Add the cumin and coriander and toss in the lentils. Stir well and heat through. Season to taste with salt and black pepper. Add the freshly cooked noodles and gently mix. Heat through over a low flame. Transfer the mixture to a warmed serving dish and sprinkle grated cheese over the top.

Variation

Layer the onion mixture, lentils and noodles or spaghetti in a baking dish and pour a tomato sauce (see index) over the dish. Sprinkle grated cheese over the top and bake in a preheated oven at 375°F (190°C, gas mark 5) for 30 minutes.

Recommended supplementary dish: Basic mixed salad (for recipe see index).

Vegetable Kichiri   *Serves 4*

The English breakfast dish kedgeree was derived from this Indian recipe in which lentils, rice and vegetables are cooked together in one pot.

2 tablespoons vegetable oil
1 medium onion, thinly sliced
1 medium carrot, grated
8 oz (225 g) long grain brown rice, washed, drained
4 oz (100 g) green *or* brown lentils, soaked overnight, drained
2 tablespoons dessicated coconut, lightly dry roasted
1 teaspoon cumin seeds

1 teaspoon powdered cinnamon
½ teaspoon ground turmeric
¼ teaspoon ground cloves
1½ pt (850 ml) water, boiling
salt to taste

Garnishing
1 banana, sliced
2 oz (50 g) roasted almonds *or* peanuts

Heat the oil in a large pan and sauté the onions until just soft, add the carrots and continue sautéing until the onions are coloured light brown. Put in the rice and lentils and fry over a low heat, stirring, for 5 minutes. Add the coconut and spices, mix well and cook, stirring for a further 2 minutes. Pour in the water, mix, season to taste with salt. Reduce the heat to as low as possible, cover the pan and simmer for 45 to 50 minutes or until all the liquid is absorbed and the rice and lentils are tender. Serve garnished with slices of bananas and roasted almonds or peanuts.

Recommended supplementary dishes: Chickpeas in yoghurt and wholemeal chapattis (for recipes see index).

Red Bean and Burgundy Casserole *Serves 6*

A rich and filling casserole with a tempting aroma. This is a good dish to serve at a dinner party on a cold winter's night.

2 tablespoons vegetable oil
2 medium onions, coarsely chopped
2 cloves garlic, crushed
2 teaspoons cumin seeds
1 teaspoon dried oregano
18 oz (500 g) cooked red kidney beans (about 6 oz/175 g when dry)
6 oz (175 g) brown *or* green lentils, soaked in cold water for 1 hour, drained
4 medium potatoes, peeled and cut into large chunks
10 fl oz (350 ml) red wine

16 fl oz (450 ml) water
1 bay leaf
1 teaspoon dried thyme
14 oz (400 g) tinned tomatoes
8 oz (225 g) carrots, peeled, sliced
1 small cauliflower, broken into florets
5 oz (150 g) button mushrooms, sliced
8 oz (225 g) leeks, sliced
salt and black pepper

Garnishing
finely chopped parsley

Heat the oil in a large saucepan, add the onion and cook until soft. Add the garlic, cumin and oregano and cook for a further 2 minutes. Add the kidney beans, lentils, potatoes, wine, water, bay leaf and thyme. Simmer for 10 minutes, then add the tomatoes and carrots. Cook for another 10 minutes and add the cauliflower. Again, after 10 minutes add the mushrooms and leeks and simmer for a further 10 minutes. Season with salt and pepper and sprinkle the parsley over.

Recommended supplementary dishes: Wholemeal bread or French wholemeal bread and a basic mixed salad (for recipes see index).

Chickpea and Vegetable Curry   *Serves 6*

2 tablespoons vegetable oil
1 large onion, chopped
2 cloves garlic, crushed
2 teaspoons ground cardomom
1 teaspoon ground cumin
½ teaspoon chilli powder *or*
    hot pepper sauce
2 teaspoons ground turmeric
8 oz (225 g) carrots, sliced
4 sticks celery, sliced
1-in (2·5-cm) piece fresh ginger
    root, grated *or* 1 teaspoon ground
    ginger

5 fl oz (150 ml) vegetable stock *or*
    water
5 fl oz (150 ml) natural low fat
    yoghurt
salt and black pepper
4 oz (100 g) button mushrooms,
    rinsed
12 oz (350 g) cooked chickpeas,
    drained (4 oz/100 g dried
    chickpeas)
2 oz (50 g) dessicated coconut,
    lightly toasted until golden

Melt the oil in a saucepan, add the onion and garlic and cook until soft. Add the cardomom, cumin, chilli and turmeric and cook, stirring continuously, for 5 minutes. Add the carrots and celery and mix well. Stir in the ginger, stock and yoghurt. Season to taste with salt and black pepper, bring to a very low simmer, cover and cook gently for 30 minutes. Add the mushrooms and chickpeas and continue cooking for 10 minutes. Sprinkle coconut over the dish and serve.

Recommended supplementary dishes: Brown rice, wholemeal chapattis, and low fat natural yoghurt.

Chilli Beans   *Serves 6*

This is like a mild chilli con carne without the meat. Serve with grated cheese sprinkled over the top.

1 tablespoon vegetable oil
1 small onion, chopped
2 cloves garlic, crushed
1 dried chilli, seeded and finely
    chopped *or* 1–2 teaspoons chilli
    sauce
14 oz (400 g) canned tomatoes,
    drained and chopped
½ teaspoon honey

½ teaspoon ground cumin
½ teaspoon dried oregano
½ teaspoon dried basil
½ teaspoon ground coriander
salt and black pepper
1½ lb (700 g) cooked kidney beans,
    drained (8 oz/225 g dry weight)
2 tablespoons cracked wheat
4 fl oz (100 ml) water

Heat the oil in a saucepan, add the onions, garlic, and chilli. Cook until soft, then add the tomatoes, honey, cumin, oregano, basil, coriander and season with salt and pepper. Cook gently for 5 minutes. Add the beans, cracked wheat and water. Bring to the boil, cover and simmer for 30 to 45 minutes or until thick, stirring occasionally.

Recommended supplementary dishes: Cooked grain, green salad and wholemeal bread or tortillas (for recipes see index).

Chickpeas Spanish Style   *Serves 4*

1 lb (450 g) chickpeas, soaked
   overnight, drained
2 pt (1·1 litres) water
3 tablespoons vegetable oil (olive oil
   if possible)
1 medium onion, diced
3 cloves garlic, crushed
1 medium green pepper, chopped

1 lb (450 g) fresh *or* tinned
   tomatoes, chopped
½–1 dried *or* fresh chilli, finely
   chopped *or* ½–1 teaspoon hot
   pepper sauce
1 tablespoon fresh parsley, chopped
salt to taste

Put the chickpeas, water and 1 tablespoon oil in a large saucepan and bring to the boil, cover, reduce heat and set to simmer. Meanwhile sauté the onion and garlic until golden in the remaining oil in a frying pan. Add the green pepper and cook until soft. Add the remaining ingredients to the frying pan, stir well, and gently simmer the mixture for 20 to 30 minutes. As the chickpeas approach tenderness (after about 1 hour) add this tomato sauce to them and continue cooking until the chickpeas are tender. Serve.

Recommended supplementary dishes: Kasha (buckwheat) or brown rice and protein plus coleslaw salad (for recipes see index).

Virginia Black-eyed Beans   *Serves 4*

A very simple but tasty bean dish to be served with the complementary protein dish suggested.

1 lb (450 g) black-eyed beans,
   soaked overnight and drained
1 medium onion, quartered
½ teaspoon dried thyme
1 bay leaf

2 whole cloves
¼ teaspoon black pepper
water
salt to taste

Put the beans, onion, thyme, bay leaf, cloves and black pepper into a heavy saucepan. Just cover with water and bring to the boil. Cover, reduce the heat and simmer for 1 to 1½ hours or until peas are very tender. Season to taste with salt and serve. During the cooking time, check occasionally and add water as required.

Recommended supplementary dishes: Brown rice and baked corn on the cob (for recipes see index).

Sunflower Seed, Soya Bean and
Almond Casserole   *Serves 4*

An unusual but delicious combination of protein foods.

8 oz (225 g) soya beans soaked
   overnight in
2 pt (1·1 litres) water
2 medium carrots, diced
1 medium onion, chopped
1 tablespoon honey
2 oz (50 g) sunflower seeds

1 teaspoon dill seeds
2 tablespoons chopped parsley
2 tablespoons soy *or* Worcestershire
   sauce
salt and pepper to taste
2 oz (50 g) flaked almonds

Put the beans and soaking water into a pot and bring to the boil, reduce the heat, cover and simmer until the beans are tender (about 3 hours). Drain the beans and reserve the liquid. Preheat the oven to 375°F (190°C, gas mark 5) and lightly grease a 3½-pt (2-litre) casserole dish with lid. Put the drained beans and the remaining ingredients except the almonds into the casserole dish and add 8 fl oz (225 ml) of the reserved liquid. Cover and bake in the preheated oven for 50 minutes. Remove the dish from the oven and sprinkle the flaked almonds over. Return to the oven, uncovered, and bake for a further 15 minutes. Serve.

Recommended supplementary dish: Greek salad (for recipe see index).

Beancurd Burgers   *Serves 4*

Delicious, protein–rich, low fat burgers.

4 tablespoons vegetable oil
½ medium onion, finely diced
1 small green pepper, cored, seeded
   and finely diced
1 medium carrot, grated
12 oz (350 g) beancurd, drained

2 tablespoons wholemeal flour
1 egg, beaten
4 oz (100 g) cheese, grated
salt to taste
wholemeal flour for dusting

Heat half the oil in the frying pan and add the onion, pepper and carrot. Stir fry until the onion is softened. Mash the beancurd in a mixing bowl and add the fried vegetables, flour, eggs, cheese and salt. Mix well and then, with wet hands, form the mixture into about 12 small burger shapes. Dust them with flour and fry them brown on both sides in the remaining oil.

Recommended supplementary dishes: Apple and celery salad with curry dressing and wholemeal pitta bread (for recipes see index).

Haricot Bean Goulash   *Serves 4*

4 tablespoons vegetable oil
1 clove garlic, crushed
2 medium onions, thinly sliced
8 oz (225 g) mushrooms, sliced
1 tablespoon tomato purée
1 lb (450 g) haricot beans, soaked
   overnight, drained
16 fl oz (450 ml) water *or* vegetable
   stock, boiling

1 tablespoon paprika
½ teaspoon dry English mustard
pinch cayenne
1 teaspoon caraway seeds
¼ teaspoon black pepper
1 bay leaf
salt to taste

Preheat the oven to 325°F (170°C, gas mark 3). Heat the oil in a heavy casserole dish, add the garlic and the onions and sauté until golden. Add the remaining ingredients, except for the salt, and mix well. Cover, bring to the boil and transfer to the oven. Bake for 2 to 3 hours or until the beans are tender. Salt to taste and serve.

Recommended supplementary dish: Wholemeal spaghetti or noodles or wholemeal bread and a green salad (for recipes see index).

Italian Beans   *Serves 4*

1 lb (450 g) haricot beans, soaked
   overnight, drained
1 clove garlic, crushed
1 small onion, thinly sliced
1 medium green pepper, cored,
   seeded, thinly sliced
2 tablespoons tomato purée
16 fl oz (450 ml) water

2 tablespoons olive oil
2 tablespoons fresh parsley,
   chopped
8 green olives, stoned, chopped
salt to taste
4 oz (100 g) Parmesan *or* Cheddar
   cheese, grated

Preheat the oven to 325°F (170°C, gas mark 3). Combine beans with all the ingredients except the cheese and salt and place them in a heavy casserole dish. Cover and bring to the boil. Transfer to the oven and bake for 2 hours. Salt to taste and sprinkle cheese over the top. Bake uncovered for a further 30 minutes or until the cheese melts and browns.

Recommended supplementary dishes: Wholemeal spaghetti or noodles or wholemeal bread and a green salad.

Aduki Bean Hotpot   *Serves 4*

This dish combines beans, oats and fruit. It's tasty, well balanced and nutritious.

12 oz (350 g) aduki beans
2 pt (1·1 litres) water
4 oz (100 g) carrots, chopped
2 medium onions, chopped
4 sticks celery, chopped

2 tablespoons oil
2 apples, thinly sliced
2 bay leaves
salt and pepper to taste
3 oz (75 g) oats, pre-soaked

Soak the beans in the water for 2 to 3 hours and then gently boil in the same water for 1 hour. Sauté the onions, carrots and celery in the oil until just soft. Add the sautéed vegetables, the apple, bay leaves and seasoning to the beans and their cooking water. Bring the mixture to the boil and simmer for 30 minutes. Drain the oats and add them to the pot, simmer for a further 10 minutes and serve.

Recommended supplementary dish: Brown rice.

Boston Baked Beans on Spanish Toast   *Serves 4*

This well-known bean dish is simple to prepare and a distinct improvement on 'beans on toast'! It is a complete meal in itself.

1 lb (450 g) haricot beans, soaked
  overnight and drained
2 tablespoons vegetable oil
2 medium onions, chopped
3 tablespoons molasses
4 tablespoons tomato purée
1 tablespoon French mustard (*or*
  other mild mustard)
salt to taste

Toast
4 slices brown bread, toasted
butter for spreading over toast
4 eggs, separated
4 oz (100 g) Gruyère cheese,
  grated
pinch of cayenne pepper
salt and black pepper

To prepare the beans

Cover the beans with water in a pot and cook until tender (about 1½ hours). Drain the beans and reserve the liquid. Preheat the oven to 350°F (180°C, gas mark 4). In a casserole dish (9–12 in/23–30 cm in diameter) heat the oil and sauté the onion until softened. Add the drained beans, 8 fl oz (225 ml) of the cooking liquid and the remaining ingredients. Mix well, cover and cook in the preheated oven for 20 minutes, uncover the dish and cook for a further 20 minutes.

To make the toast

Preheat the oven to 400°F (200°C, gas mark 6). Butter the toast and put it onto a baking sheet. Place one egg yolk onto each slice of toast. Whisk the egg white lightly, beat in the cheese and spread it gently over the top of the yolk, covering the toast completely. Season with cayenne, salt and pepper. Bake in the preheated oven for 10 to 15 minutes or until golden brown, then serve with the beans.

Red Bean Stuffed Tortillas   *Serves 4*

Tortillas are thin pancakes made with a corn flour dough (see index for preparation). They are served here with a kidney bean filling and covered with tomato sauce. Stuffed tortillas are known as tacos.

2 tablespoons vegetable oil
1 small onion, coarsely chopped
½ green pepper, cored, seeded,
  coarsely chopped
1 small dried chilli, seeded, finely
  chopped
1 clove garlic, crushed
1 lb (450 g) cooked kidney beans
  (6 oz/175 g dried), drained
6 fl oz (175 ml) tomato sauce (see
  page 112)

1 teaspoon chilli powder
½ teaspoon ground cumin
salt and black pepper
8 cooked tortillas (shop–bought *or*
  for preparation see page 94)
¼ head of lettuce, shredded
4 tomatoes, coarsely chopped
4 oz (100 g) Cheddar cheese, grated

Preheat the oven to 350°F (180°C, gas mark 4). In a large saucepan heat the oil over a medium heat. Add the onions, peppers and dried chilli. Cook until tender. Add the garlic, beans, tomato sauce, chilli powder and cumin and season with salt and pepper. Cover and simmer gently over a low heat for 5 minutes. Place the tortillas on a baking sheet and bake in the preheated oven for 5 minutes. Fill each tortilla with a portion of the bean mixture. Fold them up and place two to a plate. Top with lettuce, tomatoes and cheese. Serve immediately.

Recommended supplementary dish: Basic mixed salad (for recipe see index).

Breads

Leavened (yeasted) bread

Leavened bread can be made from any sort of wheat flour, but to make bread with a fine texture and a good satisfying taste it is best to use a hard (also called strong) flour. These are flours with a high gluten content and they give a firm elastic dough. You may use either strong brown or strong white flour, depending upon your preference and the type of bread you wish to make. Stoneground 100 per cent wholemeal flour makes the most nutritious and filling bread. For a lighter, less chewy bread, but one which still retains most of the goodness of the wheat, use wheatmeal of 81 to 85 per cent extraction. For the times when you wish to make a light-textured bread, use a strong white flour of a low extraction.

There is no magic attached to bread-making, and as long as you know what you are doing and why, there is no reason why every home-baking session shouldn't be a success. Below is a simple description of the various stages involved in making bread and why they are needed.

Yeast is mixed with water and, to initiate the process that produces the gas carbon dioxide which causes the dough to rise, it is fed some sugar. The yeast/sugar mixture starts to bubble and it is then mixed with flour, a little salt and enough water to give a firm dough. The yeast enzymes start to feed on the sugar in the flour itself, the water hydrates the protein in the flour to give gluten and the salt encourages enzyme activity. The gluten forms a matrix which is expanded by the carbon dioxide to give a spongy dough full of air. After the dough is made it is kneaded; this has a two-fold purpose. Kneading improves the elasticity of the gluten and it redistributes the yeast evenly throughout the dough producing fresh sites for enzyme activity. After kneading, the dough is allowed to rise to double its original volume then punched down and shaped into loaves before being placed in tins to rise one more time. The timing here is important since if the process takes too long the dough loses its elasticity and the texture of the bread is uneven. On the other hand, if the process is cut short, the gluten remains unstretched and the bread will be heavier than it should be. In the final stage of the operation, the bread is placed in the oven to bake. The heat kills the yeast and stops further activity, expands the gas in the dough and sets the starch and proteins. This combined activity produces a firm but airy bread.

Below is a recipe for a basic wholemeal bread. Following the recipe are suggestions for other breads in which part of the wholemeal flour in the basic recipe is replaced by other flours.

Basic Wholemeal Bread

This bread keeps well, and it can be used up to one week after baking. All wholemeal flours do not bake in the same way, so do experiment with different brands of flour (and with the given recipe) until the bread you make is exactly to your liking. This is a basic bread recipe for two loaves of about 1 lb (450 g) each.

2 teaspoons brown sugar	1 tablespoon salt
¾ oz (20 g) fresh yeast *or* 1 level tablespoon active dried yeast	1 tablespoon vegetable oil cracked wheat or sesame seeds
¾ pt (425 ml) slightly warm water	(optional)
1½ lb (700 g) wholewheat flour	1 tablespoon melted butter

Mix the sugar, yeast and a little of the water into a smooth paste in a small bowl and set aside in a warm place until the mixture has frothed up (approximately 15 minutes). Put the flour and salt into a large mixing bowl, add the yeast mixture, oil and remaining water. Knead the mixture until you have a smooth springy dough that comes away from the sides of the bowl. Turn the dough onto a floured board and knead well for about 5 minutes (longer if you have strong arms). Wash, dry and slightly grease the mixing bowl, place the dough in it, cover the bowl with a warm damp cloth and set it aside in a warm place for 1 to 1½ hours or until the dough has risen to double its original size. Knead the dough again for 5 minutes and then divide it into 2 equal parts. Shape the dough pieces and place them into two lightly buttered 1-lb (450-g) bread tins. Sprinkle the cracked wheat or sesame seeds on to the top of each loaf, cover the tins with a warm, damp cloth and leave them in a warm place for 30 to 45 minutes, or until the dough has risen to the top of the tins. Preheat the oven to 450°F (230°C, gas mark 8), place the tins in the centre of the oven and bake for 40 minutes. Remove the bread from the oven, tip the loaves out of the tins and knock the underside. If the bread sounds hollow like a drum it is cooked. If the bread does not sound hollow, return the loaves, upside down, to the oven and bake for a further 10 minutes at 375°F (190°C, gask mark 5). Leave the bread to cool on a wire rack, or resting across the top of the empty bread tins.

Variations:

To prepare a variety of different breads you may partially replace the wholewheat flour in the above recipe with the following substitutes in the amounts suggested. (The comments in brackets describe the probable differences between bread made with the basic recipe and breads with the substitutes.)

8 oz–1 lb (225 g–450 g) unbleached white flour (lighter)

4 oz–8 oz (100 g–225 g) cornmeal (slightly crunchier)

8 oz–12 oz (225 g–350 g) rye flour (more moist and compact)

4 oz (100 g) buckwheat flour (stronger flavour)

4 oz–8 oz (100 g–225 g) soya flour (adds to the protein content and gives more flavour)

4 oz–8 oz (100 g–225 g) oat flour or rolled oats (adds to the protein content, chewier and more moist)

High Protein Bread

In this recipe, which is another variation of the basic wholemeal bread recipe, a portion of the wholemeal flour is replaced by a mixture of ingredients rich in protein, vitamins and minerals. The finished bread is close-grained, easy to slice and excellent for sandwiches or toast.

Replace the wholemeal flour in the basic wholemeal bread recipe with the following mixture:

1 lb (450 g) wholemeal flour
2 oz (50 g) non-instant dried
   skimmed milk
2 oz (50 g) soya flour

1 oz (25 g) wheat germ
1 oz (25 g) rolled oats soaked in
   4 fl oz (100 ml) boiling water and
   allowed to cool

Combine the ingredients in a mixing bowl and stir well, then proceed as directed in the wholemeal bread recipe.

Wholemeal Bread Rolls   *Makes 10 rolls*

Follow the basic wholemeal bread recipe up to the stage where the dough has risen once and has been kneaded – a second time – for 5 minutes. Now weigh out the dough into 3-oz (75-g) pieces and shape each piece into a smooth ball. Place the rolls onto a lightly buttered baking sheet (or sheets) and cover them with a clean, slightly damp cloth. Leave the rolls to rise in a warm place for 35 to 40 minutes. Preheat the oven to 450°F (230°C, gas mark 8). Put the rolls in the oven and bake for 10 to 15 minutes or until browned to your taste.

Herb Rolls   *Makes 20 rolls*

12 oz (350 g) strong white flour
5 oz (150 g) wholemeal flour
2 oz (50 g) cracked wheat
1 teaspoon salt
½ oz (15 g) caraway seeds
2 tablespoons fresh herbs, e.g.
 parsley, basil, thyme, finely
 chopped

1 clove garlic, crushed well
12 fl oz (350 ml) milk
1 oz (25 g) fresh yeast *or* 1 level
 tablespoon active dried yeast
1 egg, beaten

Combine the white flour, 4 oz (100 g) of the wholemeal flour and 1 oz (25 g) of the cracked wheat, salt, caraway seeds, herbs and garlic in a large mixing bowl. Pour the milk into a saucepan and heat through gently until just tepid, neither too warm nor too cold to the touch Add the yeast and mix well until dissolved. Add this mixture to the flours and mix well until the dough leaves the sides of the bowl. Turn the dough onto a lightly floured surface and knead for 5 to 10 minutes until you have a smooth, elastic dough. (Or: place flours into the bowl of a food processor and, with the machine running, pour the yeast liquid through the feed tube and process until the mixture forms a ball around the knife, and then for another 15 to 20 seconds to knead the dough.) Place the dough in the mixing bowl, cover with a damp cloth and leave it to rise in a warm place for 45 minutes to 1 hour, until it has doubled in bulk.

Preheat the oven to 425°F (220°C, gas mark 7). Punch the dough down with your fists and knead lightly. Using a lightly floured board cut the dough into 20 equal portions and shape each one into a roll. Place rolls 1 in (2·5 cm) apart on a lightly greased baking sheet. Brush with the beaten egg and sprinkle with a mixture made from the remaining cracked wheat and wholemeal flour. Leave to rise for 10 to 15 minutes and then bake the rolls in the preheated oven for 15 to 20 minutes or until golden brown. (Tap the base of a roll; if it sounds hollow, it will be cooked.)

These rolls can be cooled quickly and frozen. To reheat, place in a moderate oven for 5 minutes.

Wholemeal Pitta Bread   *15 pitta breads*

Pitta bread is round and flat with a hollow in the middle. The texture is soft, even on the outside and it is delicious for eating with dips such as hummus or for mopping up sauces. In the Middle East, where pitta bread is a staple food, it is served stuffed with salads and/or cooked food. A very popular dish available from street corner stalls is pitta bread filled with falafel (small deep fried balls made from ground chickpeas) and topped with a spicy sauce.

Pitta dough is leavened but the baking time is very short and at a high temperature. During baking the dough magically separates, giving the important pouch or hollow in the middle of the bread. In Jerusalem I visited a small pitta bakery run by a Syrian where he made the very large and slightly crisp Syrian pitta bread. They were baked in a dome-shaped oven with a wood fire in the bottom. The flat, circular dough shapes were stuck onto the inside surface of the domed oven roof and baked for just 2 to 3 minutes by which time they were just about to fall into the flames below. Just in the nick of time the Syrian would reach into the oven with a long spatula, catch them and deliver them to the counter, truly freshly baked.

½ oz (12.5 g) fresh yeast *or* 1 level
    teaspoon active dried yeast
2 fl oz (50 ml) warm water
1 teaspoon sugar

1 lb (450 g) wholemeal flour
½ teaspoon salt
10 fl oz (275 ml) water
    (approximately)

Mix the yeast, warm water and sugar into a smooth paste in a small bowl and set it aside in a warm place for 15 minutes or so until the mixture has frothed up. Sift the flour and salt into a mixing bowl and pour in the yeast mixture. Knead by hand and slowly add the water to form a firm dough, neither too hard nor too soft. Turn the dough onto a floured board and knead it for 10 to 15 minutes. This is vital if the bread is to have the right texture. Lightly grease a large bowl, place the dough in it and leave it in a warm place for 1½ to 2 hours or until doubled in size. Knead the dough again for 2 to 3 minutes then divide it into 15 equal portions. Form them into balls and roll them into circles ¼ in thick on a floured board. Dust each round with flour and set to rise again on a floured cloth in a warm place for about 20 minutes. Meanwhile pre-set the oven to 450°F (230°C, gas mark 8). After 10 minutes place 2 ungreased baking sheets in the oven to warm up. Lightly sprinkle the dough rounds with cold water and load onto the hot baking sheets. Place them in the oven and bake for about 8 minutes. Do not open the oven door during this time. The finished pitta bread should be soft and white with a hollow in the middle. Serve as they are, or cut them crosswise at the middle or the top and stuff them with whatever filling you have ready. Store the uneaten bread in plastic bags in the freezer. To reheat, place in the oven at 350°F (180°C, gas mark 4) for 3 to 5 minutes. If this recipe makes more pitta bread than you need, divide the dough in half and make one half into a normal loaf. Baking instructions are given in the basic wholemeal bread recipe.

Wholemeal French Bread

These amounts will make two loaves of about 1 lb (450 g) each.

4 fl oz (100 ml) warm water
4 fl oz (100 ml) warm milk
4 fl oz (100 ml) natural yoghurt
¾ oz (20 g) fresh yeast *or* 1 level tablespoon active dried yeast

1 tablespoon sugar
1½ lb (700 g) wholemeal flour
1 teaspoon salt
1 tablespoon melted butter

Combine the water, milk, yoghurt, yeast and sugar in a mixing bowl. Stir well and leave in a warm place for 15 minutes or until the mixture is frothy. Add the salt and half the flour and beat the mixture into a smooth dough. Add the remaining flour and mix it in. Knead the dough in the bowl until it has lost any stickiness and then turn it out onto a floured board and knead it for a further 5 to 10 minutes. The finished dough should be firm and quite stiff; add a little more flour if it is not. Wash, dry and slightly grease the mixing bowl. Put the dough back in, cover with a clean cloth and leave it to rise for 1 hour or until doubled in size. Punch the dough down and divide it in half. Roll each portion out into a large square (about 12 in (30 cm) across) on a floured board. Fold two opposite sides of a square into the middle, then fold this in half lengthways. Press all the edges together so that no seams are visible. Repeat for the other square. Lightly butter two baking sheets and place a loaf on each, cover it with a clean cloth and leave to rise in a warm place for 1½ hours or until doubled in size. Preheat the oven to 425°F (220°C, gas mark 7). Make four or five diagonal cuts about ½ in (1 cm) deep in the top of each loaf and then lightly brush each with a little cold water (to give a crunchy texture to the crust). Put the loaves in the middle or the lower middle of the oven and bake for 30 to 35 minutes (longer if the loaves are thick rather than long). After 15 minutes baking, brush the loaves once more with a little water.

Sally's Nut Bread

This is a close-textured, high protein bread.

8 oz (225 g) plain strong white
  flour
8 oz (225 g) 100% granary flour
1 teaspoon bicarbonate of soda
1 teaspoon salt

4 oz (100 g) Brazil nuts, finely
  chopped
½ pt (300 ml) plain low fat yoghurt
a few extra Brazil nuts, halved, to
  decorate

Preheat the oven to 400°F (200°C, gas mark 6). Grease a baking sheet about 10 in × 8 in (21 cm × 20 cm). Mix the flours, soda, salt and nuts together in a large bowl. Stir in the yoghurt and mix well to form a soft dough. Knead the dough on a floured surface for 2 to 3 minutes, then make it into a loaf shape and put it on the baking sheet. Decorate with halved Brazils and bake in the preheated oven, until firm and brown. Turn it out and leave to cool on a wire rack.

Rye Bread

The texture and flavour of this bread depends on whether you use light or dark rye flour. The latter gives a stronger tasting, heavier bread. These amounts make two 1-lb (450-g) loaves.

12 oz (350 g) light *or* dark rye flour
12 oz (350 g) wholemeal flour
1 tablespoon caraway seeds
2 teaspoons salt
¾ oz (20 g) fresh yeast *or* 1 level
  tablespoon active dried yeast

¾ pt (425 ml) warm water
1 tablespoon honey *or* sugar
2 tablespoons melted butter *or*
  vegetable oil

Combine the rye flour, wheat flour, caraway seeds and salt in a large mixing bowl and set them aside in a warm place. Add the yeast to the warm water, stir in the sugar and melted butter or oil. Whisk well together and set aside in a warm place for 5 to 10 minutes. Pour the yeast mixture into the flours and beat to form a smooth dough. Add a little flour if the dough is too soft. Turn the dough onto a floured board and knead for about 5 minutes. Clean the mixing bowl and lightly grease. Put the dough inside and cover with a warm, damp cloth. Leave to rise in a warm place for 1 to 1½ hours. Divide the dough in half. Grease 2 1-lb (450-g) bread tins and pack half the dough in each. Cover again and set aside in a warm place for 30 to 40 minutes or until the dough has doubled in size. Preheat the oven to 375°F (190°C, gas mark 5). Bake for 45 minutes or until the loaves are quite browned. The baking time may be longer if you have used dark rye flour.

Rye Rolls *Makes 10 rolls*

Prepare the dough as above. Pinch out 3-oz (75-g) pieces of dough after the first rising and form them into balls. Place them on a greased baking sheet and leave them to rise until doubled in size (about 1 to 1½ hours). Bake them in a preheated oven at 350°F (180°C, gas mark 4) for 30 to 35 minutes.

Unleavened (unyeasted) bread

Unleavened or unyeasted bread is made by mixing flour, salt and water to form a dough which is shaped into a loaf or rolled out into a flat round and baked. In the past, since it can be cooked more quickly than leavened bread, this type of bread has been more common in areas of the world where fuel was not easily available. In recent times it has become more widely popular, and is particularly recommended by the macrobiotic movement.

In India and Pakistan, the most common form of bread is the flat, unleavened, round chapatti. The wheat grain is ground locally on stone mills, and the flour produced is quite coarse. In the West, special chapatti flour can be obtained from Indian provision stores.

Another well-known unleavened bread is the tortilla from Mexico. It is made from a cornmeal and wholemeal wheat flour mixture. Recipes for chapattis and tortillas are given below.

Basic Unleavened Bread

Unyeasted bread is heavier than the risen variety, so it is worth cutting it in thin slices and chewing it well. The recipe given here is a very simple one but it can be varied by replacing half the wheat flour with other flours (e.g. buckwheat, cornmeal, rice, soya, millet or rye flour, etc.) or combinations of flours (see below). For a sweet bread add chopped nuts and dried fruit to the ingredients. To make a bread that will double as a meal, try adding left-over cooked vegetables or grains to the dough mix and then serve slices of the baked bread with a spicy sauce. These amounts will make two 1-lb (450-g) loaves.

1½ lb (700 g) 100% wholemeal flour
2 teaspoons salt
warm water (about ¾ pt/425 ml)

Combine the flour and salt in a mixing bowl and slowly stir in the warm water until you have a firm dough that comes away from the sides of the bowl. Knead the dough with vigour on a floured board for as long as you have the patience (at least 10 minutes). The more you knead the dough the better will be the texture of the finished bread. Form the dough into a ball, lightly oil your hands with the vegetable oil and run them over the ball. Clean and dry the mixing bowl and place the dough in it. Cover it with a clean cloth and set it aside in a warm place for 24 to 36 hours. About every 8 hours, punch the dough down and turn it over. Divide the dough in half and place each half in a lightly oiled 1-lb (450-g) bread tin. Cover and set aside in a warm place for another 3 to 5 hours. Preheat the oven to 300°F (150°C, gas mark 2). Place the bread in the oven and bake for 1½ hours or until the loaves slip easily out of the tins and sound hollow when tapped. Allow them to cool before using. Store unused bread wrapped in cling film in the refrigerator.

Variations:

Replace the wholemeal flour in the recipe by one of the following flour mixtures:

or

1 lb (450 g) wholemeal flour
4 oz (100 g) rye flour
4 oz (100 g) cornmeal

1 lb (450 g) wholemeal flour
4 oz (100 g) bulgar wheat flour
4 oz (100 g) cornmeal

Tortillas   *Makes 10*

Tortillas are served with hot, spicy dishes, especially bean dishes. Beans and tortillas make a good complementary protein combination.

4 oz (100 g) 100% wholemeal flour
4 oz (100 g) cornmeal
2 oz (50 g) soft margarine
pinch salt
hot water

Combine the flour, cornmeal, margarine and salt and mix well to form a coarse meal. Add the hot water slowly to form a firm dough that does not stick to the sides of the bowl. Pinch off about 10 pieces of dough and roll them into balls. Flatten the balls and roll them out on a floured board into rounds about 6 in (15 cm) in diameter. Heat an ungreased frying pan over a moderate flame and cook 1 or 2 tortillas at a time. Turn them frequently until they are flecked with brown on both sides. Remove them to a moderate oven to keep warm and cook the remaining tortillas. Cold tortillas may be reheated by the same method.

Chapattis

Makes 8

This Indian bread is normally eaten with curried food or other Indian-style savoury dishes.

8 oz (225 g) 100% wholewheat
  flour
2 tablespoons vegetable oil
½ teaspoon salt
water (about 6 fl oz/175 ml)

Mix the flour, oil, salt and water in a bowl to form a fairly stiff dough that comes away from the side of the bowl. Knead the dough until the texture is smooth and elastic, pinch off 8 pieces and roll them into balls. Flatten the balls on a floured board roll them out thinly into circles approximately 8 in (20 cm) in diameter. Heat an ungreased heavy frying pan over a high flame. Place a chapatti in it, cook the chapatti for about 1 minute and then turn it over. Press the edges with a spatula; they should puff up slightly. Continue cooking until the underside is just mottled with brown spots. Remove the chapatti from the pan and store it in a heated oven or wrap in a clean cloth to keep it warm while you cook the others.

Salads

The recipes given here are divided into salads containing one or more good protein sources and those which are low in protein content. The protein salads were chosen for their flavour and also to complement the protein and the other nutrients in the main meal recipes. They all contain as a major ingredient one or more of the protein sources: grains, pulses, dairy products or nuts.

The low protein salads were chosen for their flavour, texture, and also because they are rich sources of vitamins, minerals, carbohydrates, unsaturated fats and fibre. They make excellent side dishes to meals already rich in protein and, with bread and cheese or a bean dip or spread, they constitute a light meal.

Protein salads

Chickpea and Cheddar Cheese Salad   *Serves 6*

This salad has flavour, a high protein content and interesting contrasting textures. Serve it well chilled.

3 tablespoons olive oil
juice of 1 large lemon
½ teaspoon ground cumin
12 oz (350 g) chickpeas, cooked
  (drained weight)

4 oz (100 g) Cheddar cheese, cut
  into cubes (½ in/1 cm square)
¼ cucumber, seeded, diced
1 tablespoon finely chopped parsley
salt and black pepper to taste

Put the olive oil, lemon juice and cumin into a mixing bowl and whisk them together. Add the chickpeas, cheese, cucumber and parsley and gently stir the mixture. Season to taste with salt and black pepper and stir again. Cover the bowl and chill the salad in the refrigerator before serving.

Chickpea and Cracked Wheat Salad   *Serves 4*

2 tablespoons vegetable oil
1 small onion, diced
8 oz (225 g) chickpeas, cooked
  (drained weight)
4 oz (100 g) cracked wheat *or*
  bulgar wheat
4 oz (100 g) tomato purée
8 fl oz (225 ml) boiling water
salt and black pepper to taste

Put the oil in a heavy pan, add the onion and sauté until golden. Add the chickpeas, cracked wheat and tomato purée. Mix well and pour in the boiling water. Season to taste with salt and black pepper and set to simmer for 15 minutes or until all the water is absorbed and the wheat is cooked. Serve hot or cold.

Chickpeas in Yoghurt and French Dressing   *Serves 4*

4 tablespoons vegetable oil
2 tablespoons wine vinegar *or* fresh
  lemon juice
1 clove garlic, crushed
salt to taste
4 fl oz (100 ml) low fat natural
  yoghurt

8 oz (225 g) chickpeas, cooked
  (drained weight)
1 tablespoon finely chopped fresh
  mint *or* 1 teaspoon dried mint,
  crushed

Combine the oil, vinegar or lemon juice and garlic and mix well. Season to taste with salt and beat in the yoghurt. Stir in the chickpeas and garnish with fresh mint, or crushed dried mint. Chill the salad before serving.

Variation:

Add diced green pepper and/or celery to the salad; they add a pleasant crunchy texture.

White Bean and Beetroot Salad   *Serves 4*

Any type of white bean, including haricot beans, butter (lima) beans or broad beans, may be used to make this salad. Red beans and other coloured beans are also suitable but the colour contrast with the beetroot is not so vivid and the salad not so exciting.

2 medium beetroots, cooked, diced
1 tablespoon butter
1 teaspoon vinegar (wine)
1 teaspoon honey
8 oz (225 g) white beans, cooked
  (drained weight)

salt to taste
2 tablespoons sour cream (use
  yoghurt if sour cream is
  unavailable)

Put the beetroot in a pan with the butter and gently heat. Stir the beetroot in the melted butter and add the vinegar and honey. Continue heating and stirring until the honey has melted and homogenized with the butter and vinegar. Pour this mixture over the beans, mix well and salt to taste. Chill and serve dressed with sour cream.

Haricot Beans, Broccoli and Hazelnut Salad   *Serves 4*

2 fl oz (50 ml) olive oil *or* other
  vegetable oil
3 tablespoons wine *or* wine vinegar
salt and black pepper to taste
8 oz (225 g) broccoli, lightly
  cooked and chopped

8 oz (225 g) cooked haricot beans
  (drained weight)
2 oz (50 g) hazelnuts, dry roasted
  and coarsely crushed

Combine the oil and vinegar, season to taste with salt and black pepper. Stir in the broccoli, beans and hazelnuts, chill and serve.

Red Bean, Tomato and Onion Salad   *Serves 4*

8 oz (225 g) red kidney beans,
  cooked (drained weight) (reserve
  cooking water)
2 tablespoons vegetable oil
1 medium onion, finely diced

2 cloves garlic, crushed
3 medium tomatoes, quartered
salt and black pepper to taste
1 tablespoon fresh parsley, chopped

Combine the beans with 8 fl oz (225 ml) of the water they were cooked in and set aside. Heat the oil in a heavy pan and sauté the onion and garlic until golden brown. Add the tomatoes and sauté for a further 2 or 3 minutes. Pour in the beans and cooking water, stir well and season to taste with salt and black pepper. Bring the mixture to the boil, cover, reduce the heat and simmer for 5 minutes. Leave to cool, chill in the refrigerator and then serve garnished with the chopped parsley.

Variation:

This salad may be prepared with other beans or mixtures of beans. Haricot beans, chickpeas and red beans combined are a particularly effective mixture in terms of colour and taste.

Mexican Red Bean Salad
*Serves 4 as a light meal,
6 as a side salad*

A filling salad and a meal in itself with bread. The combination of beans and cheese makes this salad a good protein source.

4 tablespoons vegetable oil
2 tablespoons wine *or* cider vinegar
8 oz (225 g) cooked red kidney
   beans (drained weight)
salt and black pepper to taste
1 small onion, diced small
1 medium green pepper, seeded,
   cored and chopped

1 medium avocado, peeled and
   cubed (optional)
2 oz (50 g) black olives
1 small lettuce
4 oz (100 g) grated cheese

Combine the oil, vinegar and red beans and season to taste with salt and black pepper. Mix well and chill in the refrigerator for 30 minutes. Stir in the beans, onion, green pepper, avocado and olives. Make a bed of torn lettuce leaves in a serving bowl and arrange the bean mixture on top. Sprinkle with grated cheese and serve.

Mixed Bean Salad
Serves 4

This is a general recipe which is useful for using up leftover cooked beans. The varieties of mixed bean salad you can make are limited only by the ingredients you have available and your imagination. I have outlined only the general method of preparing a mixed salad (or single bean) salad.

   Prepare 8 oz (225 g) of a cooked mixture of your favourite beans. Add chopped fresh vegetables. Toss in French dressing, yoghurt or sour cream. Season to taste with salt and black pepper, garnish with fresh chopped parsley, chives, spring onions or mint, and serve on a bed of lettuce or chopped spinach.

Bean Sprout and Bean Salad　　　　　　　*Serves 6*

This salad uses a combination of cooked, dried beans, lightly cooked fresh green beans and bean sprouts. Select your favourite dried beans or try chickpeas or red kidney beans. They both work well. You could also use a combination of dried beans.

8 oz (225 g) cooked beans, drained
8 oz (225 g) lightly cooked fresh
　green beans, drained
4 oz (100 g) bean sprouts
4 oz (100 g) chopped peanuts
2 sticks celery, chopped

½ medium green pepper, seeded,
　cored and diced
juice of 1 lemon
4 tablespoons vegetable oil
1 clove garlic, crushed
salt and black pepper to taste

Combine all the beans, the bean sprouts, peanuts, celery and green pepper and carefully mix together. Add the lemon juice to the oil and garlic, beat together and season to taste with salt and black pepper. Pour the dressing over the salad and serve immediately.

Lentil Salad　　　　　　　　　　　　　*Serves 4*

12 oz (350 g) green or brown
　lentils, washed
1 medium onion
2 cloves
2 bay leaves
2 cloves garlic
1 teaspoon grated lemon peel

1 medium onion, diced
2 tablespoons vegetable oil
2 tablespoons lemon juice
½ teaspoon ground cumin
2 teaspoons ground coriander
salt and black pepper to taste
olives for garnishing

Put the lentils in a heavy pot and cover them with water. Stick the cloves in the onion and add it to the pot. Add the bay leaves, whole garlic cloves and lemon peel. Bring to the boil, reduce the heat, cover and simmer until the lentils are just tender (not disintegrating). Drain the lentils; remove and discard the onion, cloves, bay leaves and garlic. Combine the lentils with the remaining ingredients, except for the olives, and set the salad aside to chill and marinate for 1 to 2 hours. Garnish with the olives and serve.

Variations:

Add other chopped vegetables to the salad, e.g. green pepper, celery, tomatoes, apple or bean sprouts.

Greek Salad *Serves 4*

1 small lettuce, leaves torn into
  bite-size pieces
4 oz (100 g) feta cheese, cut into
  small pieces
2 oz (50 g) black olives
1 firm tomato, chopped

1 tablespoon finely diced onion
¼ cucumber, sliced
3 tablespoons olive oil
juice of 1 lemon
salt and pepper to taste

Put torn lettuce leaves into a serving bowl. Add the cheese, olives, tomato, onion and cucumber, pour over the olive oil and lemon juice and season to taste with salt and black pepper. Toss well and serve.

Variation:

To improve the protein content of this salad add 4 oz (100 g) cooked chickpeas.

Tabbouleh (Bulgar Salad) *Serves 4*

Tabbouleh is a beautiful and nutritious salad. It has a sharp, refreshing flavour and is perfect for a hot summer day. In its simplest form it is served in individual lettuce-lined bowls or stuffed into pitta bread. Here we serve it piled high on a large dish and garnished with cucumber, tomatoes and olives.

8 oz (225 g) bulgar wheat, coarse
  grain
1 medium onion, finely diced
2 oz (50 g) parsley, finely chopped
salt and black pepper to taste
1 oz (25 g) fresh mint, finely
  chopped *or* 2 tablespoons dried
  mint, crushed

4 tablespoons lemon juice
4 tablespoons vegetable oil (olive oil
  if possible)
4 oz (100 g) tomatoes, thinly sliced
cucumber, thinly sliced
2 oz (50 g) olives

Cover the bulgar wheat in water, leave it to soak for 30 minutes to 1 hour. Drain and squeeze out any excess water. Thoroughly mix the bulgar wheat and onion, stir in the parsley and season to taste with salt and freshly-milled black pepper. Mix the mint, lemon juice and oil together and pour the mixture over the bulgar wheat. Carefully stir it in and finally adjust the taste to suit, with the addition of more seasoning or lemon juice. Pile the wheat on a serving dish and decorate with tomatoes, cucumber and olives, and serve.

Variation:

To increase the protein content of the salad serve it garnished with 4 oz (100 g) feta cheese, cubed.

Spiced Bulgar Wheat Salad (Bazargan) *Serves 4*

This bulgar wheat salad is less well-known than tabbouleh but more to the taste of people who like spicy dishes.

8 oz (225 g) bulgar wheat, coarse grain
4 tablespoons olive oil
1 medium onion, finely diced
2 tablespoons finely chopped fresh parsley
2 oz (50 g) pine nuts, or chopped walnuts, lightly toasted

4 oz (100 g) tomato purée
2 teaspoons dried oregano
1 teaspoon ground cumin
½ teaspoon ground allspice
¼ teaspoon cayenne
salt and black pepper to taste

Cover the bulgar wheat with plenty of cold water and leave for 1 hour. Drain and squeeze out any excess water. Put half the oil in a frying pan and lightly sauté the onion. Transfer the bulgar wheat to a large mixing bowl and stir in the onion, frying oil, unused oil and all the other ingredients. Mix well, cover and refrigerate for 4 to 5 hours before serving. This salad improves if left a day or night before use.

Potato, Walnut and Cottage Cheese Salad *Serves 4–6*

1 lb (450 g) firm potatoes, washed
2 medium, firm tomatoes, quartered and then halved
1 small onion, finely diced
2 oz (50 g) chopped walnuts
1 teaspoon dill seeds
2 tablespoons lemon juice

2 tablespoons olive oil *or* other vegetable oil
4 oz (100 g) cottage cheese
2 oz (50 g) natural low fat yoghurt
salt and black pepper to taste
fresh parsley *or* mint to garnish

Put the potatoes in their jackets into a pot. Cover with water and cook until just tender. Cool under cold water, peel and thickly slice them. Combine the potatoes with the tomatoes, onion, walnuts and dill seeds. Beat together the lemon juice, oil, cottage cheese, yoghurt, and salt and pepper to taste, to form a smooth dressing. Pour this over the potato salad and gently stir it in. Garnish with parsley or mint and serve.

Ginger and Yoghurt Rice Salad   *Serves 4*

This is an excellent salad, rich in protein and nutritious yet refreshing and light.

1 lb (450 g) cooked long grain
 brown rice, cooled
2-in (5-cm) piece fresh ginger root,
 peeled, finely chopped
8 fl oz (225 ml) low fat natural
 yoghurt

1 medium green pepper, cored,
 seeded, finely chopped
1 stalk celery, chopped
2 oz (50 g) roasted peanuts
salt to taste
cayenne to taste (optional)

Combine all the ingredients and mix well together. Leave for 1 hour before serving to give the different flavours time to mingle.

Waldorf Salad   *Serves 6–8*

3 red dessert apples, quartered,
 cored and sliced
3 stalks celery, washed and thickly
 sliced
4 oz (100 g) unsalted peanuts

2 oz (50 g) whole hazelnuts
2 oz (50 g) sultanas
4 fl oz (100 ml) low fat yoghurt
1 teaspoon lemon juice
1 tablespoon chopped parsley

In a large bowl combine the apples, celery, peanuts, hazelnuts and sultanas. Stir in the yoghurt mixed with the lemon juice. Sprinkle the parsley over and serve.

Protein Plus Coleslaw Salad   *Serves 4*

Cabbage is available most of the year at low cost and it combines well with many other ingredients to give a wide range of salads. For this recipe I have added cheese and sunflower seeds to the cabbage to give a protein-rich salad. Other suggestions for coleslaw salads are given below the recipe.

12 oz (350 g) white *or* red cabbage
 shredded
1 medium eating apple, grated
4 oz (100 g) Cheddar cheese, diced
 small
4 oz (100 g) sunflower seeds, dry
 roasted

juice of 1 lemon
3 fl oz (75 ml) vegetable oil
2 tablespoons wine *or* cider vinegar
salt and black pepper to taste

Combine the cabbage, apple, cheese and sunflower seeds in a serving bowl and mix well together. Beat together the lemon juice, oil, vinegar and salt and pepper to taste. Toss the salad in the dressing and serve.

Variations:

Replace the cheese and/or sunflower seeds with one or two of the following: grated carrot; diced green or red peppers; sultanas or raisins; chopped almonds, walnuts or other nuts; caraway seeds; roasted peanuts; cooked, drained lentils or beans; fresh orange slices or pineapple chunks.

Low Protein Salads

Basic Mixed Salad

Here are three recipes for all-purpose mixed salads. The first is a general method recipe from which you can select quantities and ingredients to suit your own needs. The second and third use similar ingredients (measured this time, so each salad serves four) but give special instructions. All three recipes are influenced by my appreciation of Middle Eastern food.

Method 1

Chopped or sliced raw vegetables served with olive oil, lemon juice, salt and pepper and lots of fresh herbs are the basis of this everyday salad. I have not given fixed amounts in this recipe, just a general outline within which you can work.

tomatoes, quartered
cucumbers, sliced *or* cut into sticks
beetroot, cooked, sliced
lettuce leaves, chopped
spring onions (scallions), chopped
mild onion, sliced

olive oil
lemon juice
salt and black pepper
fresh and finely chopped herbs, e.g.
    mint, parsley, basil, dill,
    coriander

Arrange the vegetables in a bowl, pour plenty of olive oil and lemon juice over them, season and sprinkle with a generous amount of fresh herbs. If you can wait, leave the salad for 5 minutes before serving.

Method 2

1 clove garlic
1 small lettuce, shredded by hand
1 cucumber, thinly sliced
2 tomatoes, quartered
1 bunch spring onions, chopped
1 medium mild onion, diced
1 bunch parsley, chopped
2 tablespoons fresh mint, chopped
  or 1 teaspoon dried mint

Dressing
2 fl oz (50 ml) olive oil or other
  vegetable oil
3 tablespoons lemon juice
salt and black pepper to taste

Rub the inside of a large bowl with the clove of garlic. Combine the ingredients of the dressing and add the clove of garlic, crushed. Mix well. Put the salad vegetables and the herbs into the bowl, mix well, toss with the dressing and serve.

Method 3

1 small cucumber, cubed
1 medium onion, diced
2 large tomatoes, chopped
1 small lettuce, shredded by hand
1 tablespoon fresh parsley, chopped
1 tablespoon fresh mint, chopped
  (optional)

2 fl oz (50 ml) olive oil *or* other
  vegetable oil
juice of 1 medium lemon
1 fresh or dried red chilli, finely
  chopped *or* ½–1 teaspoon hot
  pepper sauce
salt and black pepper to taste

Combine all the ingredients, mix well and serve.

Spinach, Walnut and Yoghurt Salad   *Serves 4*

1 lb (450 g) spinach, washed and
  chopped *or* 8 oz (225 g) frozen
  spinach, defrosted and drained
1 medium onion, finely diced
1 tablespoon olive oil

8 fl oz (225 ml) yoghurt
1 clove garlic, finely chopped
2 tablespoons chopped walnuts
1 teaspoon crushed dried mint (for
  garnishing)

Put the spinach and onion in a heavy pan. Cover and gently cook with no added water, until the spinach is wilted and soft (about 10 minutes). Add the oil and cook for a further 5 minutes. Combine the yoghurt and garlic and lightly toast the walnuts. Transfer the spinach and onions to a serving bowl, pour the yoghurt over them, sprinkle on the walnuts, garnish with crushed mint and serve.

Apple and Celery Salad with Curry Dressing   *Serves 4*

For a more substantial salad which will serve with bread as a light meal, add the optional ingredient, cheese.

8 oz (225 g) eating apples, cored and chopped
4 oz (100 g) celery, thinly sliced
2 tablespoons lemon juice
3 tablespoons vegetable oil

¼-¾ teaspoon curry powder
3 tablespoons natural yoghurt
salt and black pepper to taste
3 oz (75 g) Cheddar cheese, diced small (optional)

Combine the apple and celery in a serving bowl. Stir together the lemon juice, oil, curry powder and yoghurt. Add salt and black pepper to taste and pour the dressing over the apple and celery mixture. Stir in the cheese cubes, if used, and serve.

Variation:

Another good combination with this dressing is carrot and courgettes. Replace the apple and celery by 8 oz (225 g) carrots, coarsely grated and 8 oz (225 g) young courgettes, finely sliced.

Bean Sprout, Beetroot and Apple Salad   *Serves 4*

Bean sprouts are a rich source of vitamins, particularly vitamin C. They are cheap, quick to grow and available all the year round. All that is needed to grow them is a dark, relatively warm place (e.g. an airing cupboard), a jar and some beans. Most beans (and grains), as long as they are not too old to germinate, can be sprouted. The most commercially popular are mung beans; other favourites are chickpeas, kidney beans, soya beans and lentils. Bean sprouts may be used fresh in salads or sandwiches, cooked in soups, omelettes, etc., or in quick fried dishes in the Chinese manner. This recipe is quick and delicious.

4 oz (100 g) bean sprouts
1 medium beetroot, sliced
1 medium apple, sliced
2 oz (50 g) chopped nuts

juice of 1 lemon
1 tablespoon honey
1 tablespoon vegetable oil
pinch salt

Layer the bean sprouts, beetroot and apple slices in a salad bowl. Top with chopped nuts. Beat the lemon juice, honey, vegetable oil and salt together and pour over the salad. Serve immediately.

To sprout beans, grains or seeds

Place 1–2 oz (25–50 g) of beans, grains or seeds in the bottom of a large jar and half-fill it with water. The sprouts will be 6 to 8 times as bulky as the unsprouted beans, so make sure the jar is large enough. (1 oz/25 g beans will make approximately 8 oz/225 g bean sprouts.) Leave them to soak overnight and then drain the water away. Rinse the beans and drain again. A piece of cheese-cloth placed over the mouth of the jar makes this job easy. Now place the jar in a warm, dark place (about 70°F/20°C). Repeat the rinse and drain procedure 3 times a day for 3 to 5 days. The length of time before the sprouts are ready depends on the bean used and upon the stage at which you decide to harvest them. After this time mung bean sprouts will be about 2 in (5 cm) long, while sprouts from chickpeas, lentils, kidney beans and soya beans will be ½ in (1 cm) long. Spread the bean sprouts (drained) on a tray and leave in the daylight (indoors) for 2 to 3 hours. They can now be used as required. Store unused bean sprouts in a covered container in the refrigerator. They can be used fresh for up to 3 days or cooked for up to 5 days after harvesting. If you have 2 jars available for bean sprouting you will have a constant source of fresh bean sprouts available.

Carrot Salad
Serves 4

4 medium carrots, peeled and
  grated
2 oz (50 g) raisins (plumped up in a
  little hot water and drained)

2 fl oz (50 ml) fresh orange juice *or*
  3 tablespoons mayonnaise

Combine the ingredients and serve. Add a little sugar for a sweet salad or a little salt for a more savoury one. The salad dressed with orange juice obviously contains less fat than that dressed with mayonnaise.

Fresh Pea Salad
Serves 4

8 oz (225 g) shelled young peas
  (1 lb/450 g) before shelling)
¼ medium cucumber, thinly sliced
2 to 3 spring onions, chopped
4 tablespoons vegetable oil

2 tablespoons vinegar
salt to taste
4 radishes, halves
2 tablespoons fresh mint, chopped

Combine the peas, cucumber and spring onions in a salad bowl. Whisk the oil and vinegar together and season to taste with salt. Toss the salad in this dressing. Decorate the top with radish halves and garnish with chopped mint.

Fresh Broad Bean Salad   *Serves 4*

1 lb (450 g) shelled broad beans
   (about 2 lb/1 kg before shelling)
water
salt to taste
3 tablespoons vegetable oil

2 cloves garlic, crushed
juice of 1 lemon
black pepper to taste
1 tablespoon fresh parsley, chopped

Put the beans in a pan just covered with water, salt and bring to the boil. Cover, reduce heat and simmer until just tender. Drain and chill the beans. Meanwhile combine the oil, garlic and lemon juice and season to taste with salt and black pepper. Toss the beans in this dressing and serve garnished with parsley.

Flageolet Bean Salad   *Serves 4*

1½ lb (700 g) flageolet beans,
   cooked, drained (8 oz/225 g
   dried beans)

Dressing
2 tablespoons wine vinegar
4 tablespoons olive oil
½ teaspoon mustard
2 cloves garlic, crushed
2 tablespoons chopped parsley
salt and black pepper

Put all the ingredients for the dressing in a jar and cover with a tightly fitting lid. Shake well. Pour the dressing over the beans, toss to cover well and place the beans in a clean serving dish. Chill until ready to serve.

Avocado and Yoghurt Salad   *Serves 4*

2 medium ripe but firm avocados,
   peeled and chopped
8 fl oz (225 ml) natural low fat
   yoghurt
1 medium green pepper, seeded,
   cored and diced small

1 clove garlic, crushed
salt to taste
1 tablespoon pine nuts, lightly dry
   roasted (optional)

Combine the avocados, yoghurt, green pepper, garlic and salt to taste. Chill for 30 minutes in the refrigerator. Serve sprinkled with pine nuts.

Spreads and Sauces

These recipes supplement the high protein dishes and salads. The spreads, served on wholemeal bread, provide nutritious and protein-rich snacks, or when added to a salad, healthy light meals. The sauces included in this section are referred to in some of the high protein recipes and are given to accompany these dishes. You may of course also use them to enhance any dish of pulses or pasta to create a satisfying main meal.

Spreads

Peanut Butter

Good natural peanut butter is available in any wholefood shop, but if you have an electric blender or food processor it's very easy to make your own. Make more than you need and store it in an airtight jar.

roasted peanuts (to roast raw peanuts see page 44)

vegetable oil
salt

Put the desired quantity of peanuts into an electric blender and add a little oil to facilitate the blending process. Add salt to taste and switch on the machine. If the mixture proves too thick for the machine to deal with add a little more oil. The more oil you add the creamier the butter will be. For crunchy peanut butter, use only a little oil and blend the peanuts in short bursts until the texture you want is achieved. Alternatively, coarsely blend one-third of the peanuts used and mix them with a smooth, well-blended peanut butter.

Note: combined with either yeast extract (e.g. marmite) or miso or with mashed banana and lettuce, peanut butter makes delicious sandwiches. Spread slices of wholemeal bread with one of these combinations and serve open-faced or as a sandwich.

Sweet Peanut Sesame Butter   *Serves 4*

1 oz (25 g) sesame seeds, dry
   roasted
4 oz (100 g) peanut butter

1 tablespoon honey
¼ teaspoon salt

Combine the ingredients and mix well together.

Variation:

Use sunflower seeds instead of sesame seeds, or a mixture of both.

Egg, Cheese and Nut Spread   *Serves 4*

4 oz (100 g) finely chopped *or*
   ground nuts
2 eggs, hard boiled, shelled and
   chopped

4 oz (100 g) cheese, finely grated
juice of 2 lemons
salt and black pepper to taste

Combine the ingredients and beat them into a smooth paste.

Cheese Spread   *Serves 4*

4 oz (100 g) cottage cheese
2 oz (50 g) Cheddar cheese, finely
   grated
1 stalk celery, finely chopped

1 tablespoon mayonnaise
pinch cayenne pepper
salt and pepper to taste

Combine the ingredients and mix well.

Variations:

1. Replace (or add to) the celery with finely diced green or red pepper, onion or spring onions.
2. After spreading the cheese spread on bread, top it with slices of eating apple.

Miso-Tahini Spread   *Serves 2*

2 tablespoons tahini
1 tablespoon miso
2 teaspoons lemon juice

Mix together the tahini, miso and lemon juice and spread the mixture on wholemeal bread.

Tahini and Cumin Spread   *Serves 4*

4 oz (100 g) tahini
1 clove garlic, crushed
2 teaspoons lemon juice

½ teaspoon ground cumin
1 tablespoon parsley, finely
  chopped (optional)

Combine the ingredients and mix well.

Chickpea and Yoghurt Spread   *Serves 4*

8 oz (225 g) chickpeas, cooked and
  mashed
4 fl oz (100 ml) yoghurt
juice of 1 lemon

1 tablespoon finely chopped mint *or*
  1 teaspoon dried mint, rubbed
salt and black pepper to taste

Combine the ingredients and mix well together.

Chickpea and Onion Spread   *Serves 4*

½ small onion, finely diced
1 tablespoon vegetable oil
8 oz (225 g) chickpeas, cooked and
  mashed
juice of 1 lemon
1 tablespoon finely chopped parsley
  or 1 teaspoon dried parsley,
  rubbed

¼ teaspoon ground cumin
1 clove garlic, crushed (optional)
salt and pepper to taste

Sauté the onions in the oil until well softened. Combine the onion with the remaining ingredients and mix well.

Basic Bean Spread

Any leftover beans can be mashed, mixed with fresh or dried herbs, a little lemon juice or vinegar, diced celery or green pepper, tomato purée perhaps, and salt and pepper, to make a fine nutritious sandwich spread.

Sauces

Basic Tomato Sauce   *Makes about 1½ pt (850 ml)*

2 oz (50 g) butter *or* vegetable oil
1 medium onion, finely diced
2 lb (900 g) fresh *or* tinned tomatoes
  (drained)
4 cloves garlic, crushed
1 medium green pepper, seeded,
  cored and diced

2 teaspoons crushed, dried oregano
2 tablespoons fresh parsley,
  chopped
1 bay leaf
salt and pepper to taste

Melt the butter in a heavy saucepan or pour in the oil, and fry the onions over a low heat until soft. Skin fresh tomatoes by dropping them in boiling water for a minute or two, then lift them out and peel off the skin. Alternatively use tinned tomatoes, drained. In either case chop the tomatoes into small pieces and add them, with the garlic and green pepper to the onions, stir well and simmer for 10 minutes. Add the herbs and season to taste with salt and black pepper. Simmer for a further 10 minutes and allow to cool. Store in airtight jars, and pour a thin film of oil over the top of the sauce before screwing on the lid.

Variation:

For a thicker tomato sauce suitable for some types of pizza and the preparation of stuffings for vegetable and pasta dishes, add 6 oz (175 g) tomato purée with the chopped tomatoes.

Quick Tomato Sauce   *Makes about ¾ pt (425 ml)*

½ medium onion, finely diced
1 tablespoon vegetable oil
3 tablespoons tomato pureé

10 fl oz (275 ml) water
pinch of sugar
salt and black pepper to taste

Sauté the onion in the oil until well softened. Stir in the tomato purée, water, sugar and seasoning. Mix well and bring to the boil. Remove from the heat, and it is ready.

Spiced Tomato Sauce   *Makes about 1 pt (575 ml)*

2 tablespoons vegetable oil
2 cloves garlic
1 medium onion, finely diced
1 lb (450 g) tinned tomatoes plus
  juice
2 tablespoons tomato purée
1 teaspoon hot pepper sauce *or* 1
  dried red chilli pepper, finely
  chopped

½ teaspoon dried oregano
½ teaspoon ground cumin
salt to taste

Heat the oil in a heavy saucepan, add the onion and garlic and sauté until softened. Stir in the remaining ingredients, cover the pan and simmer for 30 minutes.

Béchamel Sauce   *Makes about 14 fl oz (400 ml)*

1 oz (25 g) butter
2 tablespoons finely diced onion
1 oz (25 g) wholemeal flour
10 fl oz (275 ml) milk

bay leaf
pinch of nutmeg
salt and freshly milled black pepper
  to taste

Melt the butter in a heavy saucepan over a low heat. Add the onion and sauté until softened and transparent. Stir in the flour to form a smooth paste and cook, stirring, for 2 to 3 minutes. Add the milk to the pan slowly with constant stirring. Continue cooking and stirring until the sauce thickens. Add the bay leaf, nutmeg and salt and black pepper and simmer, covered, over a very low heat for 10 minutes. Stir occasionally.

Cheese Sauce

Stir 2 oz (50 g) grated Cheddar cheese or other suitable cheese into the cooked béchamel sauce until it has melted. Serve. For extra flavour also stir in 1 teaspoon prepared English mustard.

Parsley Sauce

Stir 2 tablespoons finely chopped fresh parsley and 1 tablespoon fresh lemon juice into the cooked béchamel sauce.

Onion Sauce

Follow the béchamel sauce recipe but use a whole medium onion, finely diced, rather than the 2 tablespoons.

Tahini and Lemon Sauce   *Makes about 8 fl oz (225 ml)*

2 cloves garlic, crushed
1 teaspoon salt
4 fl oz (100 ml) tahini
2 fl oz (50 ml) water
juice of 2 lemons

Mash the garlic with the salt in a bowl. Slowly beat in the tahini, water and lemon juice in that order. Blend well, using an electric blender if you like. For a thicker or thinner sauce use less or more water and lemon juice respectively. Serve hot or cold.

This sauce is excellent just on its own with bread, or as a salad dressing. Also serve it with rice and vegetable dishes and as a dip.

Variation:

Add 4 oz (100 g) chopped walnuts with the garlic and salt.

Aubergine and Cheese Sauce   *Makes about 1 pt (575 ml)*

2 to 3 medium aubergines
2 oz (50 g) butter *or* vegetable
   margarine
1 oz (25 g) wholemeal flour

10 fl oz (275 ml) milk
4 oz (100 g) grated cheese
salt to taste
grated peel of a ½ lemon

Slit the aubergines lengthwise and sprinkle salt in the cut. Set aside for 30 minutes, then rinse and drain. Place the aubergines in a preheated oven at 375°F (190°C, gas mark 5) for 20 minutes. Peel off the skin, and chop the aubergine flesh into small pieces.

Melt the butter in a heavy pan, stir in the flour, and cook, stirring for 3 to 4 minutes. Add the aubergine flesh and beat to make a smooth mixture. Stir in the milk and cheese and gently simmer, stirring, until the cheese is melted. Add salt to taste, mix in the lemon rind, and serve hot with vegetables.

Desserts and Tea Breads

There is no particular pattern in this section. It is just a small, but varied, collection of rather delicious, not too unhealthy, desserts and sweet baked goods for you to enjoy.

Apricot and Oat Bars   *Makes 12*

5 oz (150 g) wholewheat flour
5 oz (150 g) rolled oats
5 oz (150 g) vegetable margarine *or*
   butter
2 oz (50 g) soft brown sugar

Filling
6 oz (175 g) dried apricots, chopped
2 tablespoons water
1 tablespoon lemon juice
1 tablespoon honey

Preheat the oven to 375°F (190°C, gas mark 5). Place the filling ingredients into a saucepan over a low heat and simmer gently until the apricots are very soft and the mixture is thick. Mix the flour and oats together in a large bowl and rub in the margarine. Stir in the sugar and spread half the oat mixture over a lightly greased (7 in/18 cm) square baking sheet, pressing down firmly. Cover with the apricot mixture and then the remaining oat mixture, pressing down well.

Bake in the preheated oven for 35 to 40 minutes. Cut into slices whilst warm. Allow the bars to cool before removing from the sheet.

Apricot Creams   *Serves 6*

8 oz (225 g) dried apricots, just
   covered in water and soaked
   overnight
10 oz (275 g) natural low fat
   yoghurt

2 egg whites
2 tablespoons dark brown sugar
1 tablespoon roasted hazelnuts,
   roughly chopped

Place the apricots in a saucepan with the water they were soaked in. Bring to the boil and simmer for 15 to 20 minutes or until soft. Sieve with a little of the water to form a purée, or process to a purée in a food processor. Allow the purée to cool and then stir in the yoghurt. Whisk the egg whites until stiff, add the sugar and whisk again. Fold this into the apricot purée and spoon the mixture into individual glasses. Sprinkle each with hazelnuts and chill until required.

Banana Scones   *Makes 18*

10 oz (275 g) wholemeal flour
4 oz (100 g) plain flour
4 teaspoons baking powder
2 oz (50 g) soft brown sugar

3 oz (75 g) vegetable margarine
8 oz (225 g) banana, mashed to a
  pulp
a little milk to glaze

Preheat the oven to 400°F (200°C, gas mark 6). Place the flours, baking powder and sugar in a large bowl. Rub in the margarine. Stir in the banana with 5 fl oz (150 ml) water and knead the mixture lightly. Turn the dough out onto a floured board and roll it out to a 1-in (2.5-cm) thickness. With a 2-in (5-cm) pastry cutter stamp out 18 scones. Place them onto a greased baking sheet, brush with a little milk and bake them in the preheated oven for 15 to 20 minutes or until golden brown and firm to the touch. Cool them on a wire rack.

V's Orange and Hazelnut Teabread *Makes 1 2-lb (1-kg) loaf*

6 oz (175 g) hazelnuts
1 large orange
8 oz (225 g) cottage cheese
6 oz (175 g) brown sugar

3 eggs, beaten
6 oz (175 g) wholemeal flour
1 teaspoon baking powder
1 tablespoon clear honey

Preheat the oven to 350°F (180°C, gas mark 4). Reserve a few of the hazelnuts whole for decoration and chop up the rest. Cut two thin strips of peel from the orange and cut away any pith attached to them. Reserve these for decoration. Grate the remainder of the rind. Put the cottage cheese and sugar into a bowl and beat into a cream. Add the eggs and orange rind and beat again. Sift the flour and baking powder together and fold into the mixture. Stir in the hazelnuts and put the mixture into a greased 2 lb (1 kg) bread tin. Bake in the preheated oven for 70 to 80 minutes or until nicely risen and golden brown on top. If the bread is correctly cooked the top will spring back when pressed. Turn the bread out of the tin and leave it to cool. Meanwhile cut the reserved orange peel into shreds and place in a small saucepan, just cover with water and gently boil for 5 minutes. Drain and mix the softened shreds with honey. Brush the top of the teabread with the mixture, decorate with the reserved hazelnuts and leave to cool.

V's Banana and Walnut Teabread   *Makes 1 2-lb (1-kg) loaf*

4 oz (100 g) vegetable margarine *or*
  butter
8 oz (225 g) brown sugar
2 eggs, beaten
4 bananas, mashed

8 oz (225 g) wholemeal flour
1 teaspoon baking powder
½ teaspoon salt
4 oz (100 g) chopped walnuts

Preheat the oven to 325°F (170°C, gas mark 3). Cream the margarine or butter and sugar together and then beat in the eggs and bananas. Sift the flour and baking powder together and fold into the mixture. Stir in the salt and the nuts, reserving a few for decoration. Put the mixture into a greased 2-lb (1-kg) bread tin (smooth down the top and sprinkle over the reserved nuts). Bake for 1 hour or until the bread is nicely risen and baked golden brown on top. Turn the teabread out of the tin and leave to cool.

Fruit-Topped
Uncooked Nut Cake   *Makes 1 1-lb (450-g) cake*

8 oz (225 g) oatflakes
4 oz (100 g) finely chopped nuts
1 large banana, mashed
1 medium carrot, grated
juice of 1 lemon

1 tablespoon brown sugar
2 tablespoons treacle
water, milk *or* cream
fresh fruit in season for the topping
  or tinned fruit, drained

Combine all the ingredients except the water, milk or cream and fruit. Mix well and then add enough water, milk or cream to form the mixture into a moist sticky consistency. Press the mixture into a round, shallow serving dish and decorate the top with fruit pieces. Chill and serve with fresh cream.

Uncooked Fruit Nut Balls   *Makes 16*

8 oz (225 g) finely chopped walnuts
8 oz (225 g) finely chopped figs
8 oz (225 g) finely chopped dates
8 oz (225 g) raisins
1 tablespoon fresh orange juice
1 teaspoon grated orange *or* lemon
  peel

Combine all the ingredients and knead into a consistent mixture. Pinch off small amounts and form into small balls. Chill before serving.

Baked Apples Stuffed with Nuts   *Serves 4*

4 large baking apples
4 oz (100 g) chopped nuts
½ teaspoon cinnamon
3 oz (75 g) brown sugar

1 tablespoon vegetable margarine *or* butter
6 fl oz (175 ml) water

Preheat the oven to 350°F (180°C, gas mark 4). Core the apples but do not peel them. Make a slight incision with a sharp knife around the middle of the apples and arrange them in a baking dish. Combine the nuts, cinnamon and half the sugar and mix well. Stuff the apples with the mixture, leaving a little mound standing proud of the apple top. Top each with a dab of margarine or butter. Dissolve the remaining sugar in the water and pour it into the baking dish. Bake the apples for 40 to 50 minutes. Serve hot or cold.

Banana Pancakes   *Serves 4*

2 eggs, beaten
½ teaspoon salt
4 oz (100 g) wholemeal flour
10 fl oz (275 ml) milk
1 tablespoon brown sugar *or* honey

2 medium-sized bananas, peeled and mashed
vegetable oil for frying
lemon juice to taste

Beat the eggs and salt together in a mixing bowl. Whisk in the flour and then the milk to form a smooth batter. Stir in the sugar or honey and bananas and beat the mixture well to eliminate any large lumps of banana. Alternatively, the ingredients of the batter could be put into the container of a food blender or processor and beaten until smooth. Brush a heavy frying pan with a little oil and heat it over a moderate flame. Pour some batter into the pan and swirl it around to form a thin ¼-in (6-mm) coating on the surface of the pan. Lightly brown the bottom side of the pancake and then turn it over and brown the other side. Repeat for the remaining batter, pile the cooked pancakes on top of one another on a buttered plate, then serve them sprinkled with lemon juice.

Date and Coconut Macaroons   *Makes 12*

4 egg whites, beaten stiff
4 oz (100 g) clear honey
8 oz (225 g) dates (use fresh ones if available) stones removed, finely chopped
12 oz (350 g) dessicated coconut

Preheat the oven to 275°F (140°C, gas mark 1). Beat the honey into the egg whites, then the dates and finally the coconut. Lightly grease a baking sheet and drop dessertspoonfuls of the macaroon mixture onto it, leaving a small space between each one. Bake in the preheated oven for 20 minutes. Allow the macaroons to cool before eating. Store unused macaroons in an air-tight tin or jar.

Fresh Fruit Compote   *Serves 4*

This recipe is from my book *Middle Eastern Vegetarian Cookery* (Rider and Company, 1982). The combination of fruit given in this recipe is only a suggestion and you may substitute any mixture of fruits or a single fruit.

4 oz (100 g) brown sugar
16 fl oz (450 ml) water
2 peaches
2 tart apples, washed
8 oz (225 g) plums, washed,
   stoned, halved

8 oz (225 g) strawberries, washed
2 sticks cinnamon *or* 1 teaspoon
   ground cinnamon
juice of 1 lemon

Put the sugar and water in a pan and bring to the boil. Set to simmer. Plunge the peaches in a pan of boiling water and then immediately remove them and drop them into cold water. The skins will now come off easily. Slice the skinned peaches and the apples and put them into the simmering syrup. Add the plums, strawberries, cinnamon and lemon juice. Simmer for 15 minutes, stirring occcasionally. Remove the cinnamon sticks (if used). Leave to cool, chill and serve with whipped cream.

Chilled Rice Pudding   *Serves 4–6*

8 fl oz (225 ml) water
1 pt (575 ml) milk
3 tablespoons brown sugar
4 oz (100 g) white rice
1 tablespoon rosewater *or* orange
   blossom water

pinch salt
ground cinnamon *or* ground ginger
   to taste (*or* both)

Put the water, milk and sugar in a heavy pan and bring to the boil. Stir in the rice, reduce the heat, cover and simmer for 45 minutes. Add the rosewater or orange blossom water and salt and simmer for a further 5 minutes. Pour the pudding into a serving dish or individual serving bowls and chill in a refrigerator. Serve sprinkled with cinnamon and/ or ginger.

Winter Fruit Salad   *Serves 4–6*

This salad is worth the effort of soaking the dried fruit overnight. The combined flavours of the prunes, apricots and port complement each other very well indeed.

8 oz (225 g) dried pitted prunes
1 pt (575 ml) strong hot tea
8 oz (225 g) dried pitted apricots
15 fl oz (425 ml) hot water
3 tablespoons honey

2 tablespoons port wine
½ orange, thinly sliced
2 tablespoons toasted flaked
   almonds
natural low fat yoghurt to taste

The day before serving cover the prunes with hot tea and the apricots with the hot water in separate bowls; leave them to soak overnight.

Combine the prunes in a pan with their soaking liquid. Sweeten with honey to taste and simmer for 20 minutes or until the prunes are tender and the syrup slightly thickened. At the same time, combine the apricots and soaking liquid in another saucepan and cook for 15 to 20 minutes, or until tender. Allow the fruits to cool and chill them thoroughly. Transfer the prunes and apricots with a slotted spoon to a serving dish. Add the port wine to the fruits and spoon a little of the apricot and prune cooking liquids over them. Decorate with very thin slices of unpeeled orange and the toasted almonds. Serve chilled with low fat yoghurt.

French Pear Tart   *Serves 4–6*

Pastry
5 oz (150 g) plain flour
5 oz (150 g) wholemeal flour
½ teaspoon salt
4 oz (100 g) butter, diced
2 oz (50 g) vegetable fat, diced
4 oz (100 g) soft brown sugar
2 oz (50 g) walnuts, finely chopped
2 egg yolks

2–4 tablespoons iced water
1 egg white, lightly beaten
2 tablespoons caster sugar

Filling
2 oz (50 g) honey
5 fl oz (150 ml) water
4 large pears, peeled, halved and
   cored

Sift the flour and salt together into a large bowl, add the fats and rub the mixture together until it resembles coarse breadcrumbs. Mix in the sugar and walnuts. Add the egg yolks and enough chilled water to bind the mixture. Meanwhile, place the honey and water in a saucepan large enough to hold all the pear halves in a single layer. Bring the syrup to the boil and simmer for 5 minutes. Add the pears to the syrup and gently simmer them for 10 to 15 minutes or until just tender. Remove them from the heat and let them cool.

Preheat the oven to 375°F (190°C, gas mark 5). Line a 9-in (23-cm) flan ring with two-thirds of the pastry. Drain the pears well and place them in the pastry case with the broad end of the pears outwards and the cut sides down. Dampen the sides of the pastry with water and then cover the flan with the remaining pastry, pressing down slightly to reveal the shape of the pears. Seal the edges and crimp all round. Cut a small hole in the centre of the flan to allow steam to escape. Brush the top of the flan with the beaten egg white and sprinkle with caster sugar. Bake in the preheated oven for 30 to 35 minutes or until the pastry is golden and firm to touch. Cool. Carefully remove from the flan ring and serve warm or cold with soured cream or yoghurt.

Nutty Pear Crumble   *Serves 4–6*

6 large pears
2 tablespoons honey
8 oz (225 g) wholemeal flour
5 oz (150 g) butter

4 oz (100 g) brown sugar
3 oz (75 g) coarsely chopped
  hazelnuts

Preheat the oven to 350°F (180°C, gas mark 4). Peel, core and thickly slice the pears. Pour a small amount of water into a saucepan, add the honey and pears. Cover and simmer gently for 5 to 10 minutes, stirring occasionally, until the pears are nearly cooked. Remove the pan from the heat and arrange the pears in a shallow baking dish. Pour over them the honey syrup from the pan. Rub together the flour and butter in a large bowl until the mixture resembles coarse bread-crumbs. Stir in the brown sugar and chopped hazelnuts. Spread the mixture evenly over the top of the pears. Bake them in the preheated oven for 45 minutes to 1 hour or until nicely browned.

Sally's Sesame Snaps   *Makes 16*

8 oz (225 g) rolled oats
3 oz (75 g) sesame seeds
8 oz (225 g) soft brown sugar

3 oz (75 g) desiccated coconut
pinch of salt
8 oz (225 g) melted butter

Preheat the oven to 350°F (180°C, gas mark 4). Mix the oats, sesame seeds, sugar, coconut and salt together in a large bowl. Stir in the melted butter and mix well. Spread the mixture evenly onto a greased baking sheet 6 × 10 in (16 × 26 cm). Bake in the preheated oven for 20 to 25 minutes or until golden brown. Allow to cool slightly and cut into 16. Carefully place them onto a wire rack to cool completely.

Part Four:
A Nutritional and Botanical Background

Grains

The grain family is comprised of over 5000 species, and amongst these can be found the world's principal cereal crops, i.e. barley, maize (corn), millet, oats, rice, rye, sorghum and wheat. (The name given to a particular cereal grass is the same as that given to its edible seeds. Thus we have the plants wheat and rice, and the seeds or grains of these plants, also called wheat and rice.) The discovery by primitive man that he could plant and harvest the seeds of these previously wild grasses led to the formation of the first village communities. They were established in fertile areas where the wild grasses were most abundant, such as the banks of the Nile and the region of Western Asia later to be called Mesopotamia.

The cultivation of cereals provided ancient communities with a food source that could be stored over long periods without becoming inedible. Thus animals could be kept and fed through the winter months and large herds could be bred. Further, in conjunction with the sowing of seasonal crops, and their storage and trade, the sciences of astronomy, mathematics and writing developed, and the earliest civilizations began to grow. The prime importance of cereal grains to these ancient cultures is reflected in many ancient traditions and myths; the name 'cereal' itself derives from Ceres, the ancient Greek and Roman goddess who was the giver of grain and life.

Until recently, particular staple grains have been associated with particular areas in the world: rice with East Asia, wheat with the West, maize (corn) with the Americas. Nowadays, with a few exceptions, these divisions are less clear and rice is as common in Europe as bread is in Japan. The exceptions stand out: sorghum and millet are, for instance, the staple grains in much of Africa, but sorghum is virtually unknown in the West, and millet only fed to budgerigars.

Cereal grains, whether eaten whole or as unrefined flour, provide an excellent nutrient balance of protein, carbohydrate, fat, vitamins, minerals and fibre.

Basic cooking methods for the common grains are given in Part Two.

DURUM.   COMMON (BREAD) WHEAT.   SPELT.   CLUB.

Wheat

Wheat, which has been called the Queen of Grains, is one of the world's most vital foods, and certainly the most widely cultivated cereal crop. It has been important to mankind since neolithic times, and has become increasingly vital as forms of wheat specifically suited to particular climatic conditions have been developed.

The success of wheat as a food crop is due to a number of factors, but two of them are particularly important. The first is the wide climatic growing range of wheat. It can be grown as far north as Alaska and as far south as the equator, and in fact it now seems possible to develop a hybrid of wheat suited to almost any habitat. The second factor is the unique quality wheat shares with rye of having a protein structure which makes its flour excellently suited to bread-making. Wheat protein has the property of forming an elastic gluten matrix when mixed with water. When yeast and sugar are added to a dough of flour and water the carbon dioxide produced is trapped by this gluten matrix, then the matrix is stretched, giving a light airy mixture that bakes into beautiful bread. Add to these properties of wheat the compact size and food value of wheat grain and its excellent storage qualities, and we have a food suited to most of humankind's needs both as an explorer and a settler.

The name 'wheat' derives from an Old German word *Weizzi*, which is similar to the Old English word *Hwoete*, both meaning 'white'. This was a description of wheat flour which, compared to other cereal flours in use in earlier times, was light in colour. There is also the English habit of calling wheat, corn. This caused me much confusion as a boy since I could never relate wheat to corn on the cob. This usage stems from the early English word *corne*, which meant staple grain. Thus the staple grain of any country was 'corne', and the first English settlers in America called the cereal crop grown by the Indians 'Indian Corne'. The Americans now call it maize, but of course the English continue to call it corn as well as calling wheat, corn.

There are thousands of species of wheat both wild and cultivated, but they all belong to the plant genus *Triticum* and of these many types, only fourteen are commonly recognized as cereal grasses. One variety, *Triticum vulgare*, which is well suited to bread-making, accounts for more than 80 per cent of wheat presently under cultivation. Apart from this, winter or Lammas wheat (*Triticum hybernum*) and spring or summer wheat (*Triticum aestivuum*) are the most widely grown for general use, and the hard-grained durum wheat (*Triticum durum*) is cultivated exclusively for the manufacture of pasta and noodles.

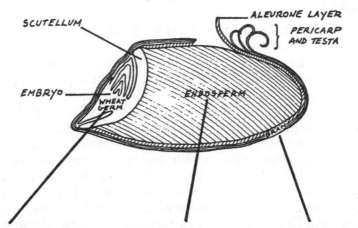

SCUTELLUM

ALEURONE LAYER

PERICARP AND TESTA

EMBRYO

WHEAT GERM

ENDOSPERM

BRAN

WHEAT GERM (3% BY WEIGHT OF WHOLE GRAIN).

CONSISTS OF THE EMBRYO OR GERM THAT CONTAINS ALL THE NUTRIENTS NEEDED TO SUSTAIN A NEW PLANT, AND THE SCUTELLUM WHICH CONNECTS THE EMBRYO TO THE ENDOSPERM. WITH THE INTRODUCTION OF STEEL ROLLERS TO FLOUR MILLING AND LATER BECAUSE OF THE NEED FOR LONG SHELF LIFE FLOURS, WHEAT GERM IS NOW OFTEN REMOVED FROM THE GRAIN DURING MILLING. THE UNSATURATED OILS PRESENT IN THE GERM CLOG UP THE STEEL ROLLERS AND CAUSE THE FLOUR TO GO RANCID. THIS PRACTICE PRODUCES A FLOUR LACKING IN NUTRIENTS SINCE THE WHEAT GERM IS PARTICULARLY RICH IN VITAMIN E, AND THE B COMPLEX VITAMINS, AND A GOOD SOURCE OF THE MINERALS CALCIUM AND IRON (SEE TABLE 3). IN SOME CIRCLES WHEAT GERM HAS A REPUTATION AS SOMETHING OF A WONDER FOOD FOR FERTILITY AND REJUVENATION!

ENDOSPERM (82% BY WEIGHT OF WHOLE GRAIN).

THIS IS THE MAIN PART IN MASS OF THE GRAIN (90%). IT IS PRINCIPALLY STARCH WITH SOME PROTEIN AND SMALL AMOUNTS OF VITAMINS AND MINERALS. THE OUTER PART OF THE ENDOSPERM BENEATH THE ALEURONE LAYER IS RICHER IN NUTRIENTS THAN THE CENTRE. THE ENDOSPERM IS USED TO MAKE WHITE FLOUR AND SEMOLINA FROM WHICH COUS-COUS AND PASTA PRODUCTS ARE MADE.

BRAN (15% BY WEIGHT OF WHOLE GRAIN).

CONSISTS OF THE TOUGH OUTER PERICARP LAYER. THE PERICARP LAYER CONTAINS LITTLE PROTEIN OR VITAMINS, BUT IT DOES PROVIDE ROUGHAGE WHICH IS NOW BEING RECOGNISED AS A NECESSARY REQUIREMENT OF A GOOD DIET. THE ALEURONE LAYER IS MOST IMPORTANT, IT CONTAINS 80% OF THE NIACIN PRESENT IN THE GRAIN, SUBSTANTIAL AMOUNTS OF THE OTHER B VITAMINS, MANY MINERALS AND A SIGNIFICANT AMOUNT (20%) OF GOOD VALUE PROTEIN (SEE TABLE 3). THE ALEURONE LAYER IS REMOVED IN VARYING AMOUNTS DURING MILLING, AND BRAN CONTAINING MUCH OF THIS LAYER WAS ONCE SOLD ONLY AS ANIMAL FOOD.

Wheat and Nutrition

The nutrient content of wheat varies widely, and more so than for other cereal grains. The percentage protein can range from 7 per cent to 20 per cent, although it is usually between 9 per cent and 14 per cent. There are many factors which govern the nutritional quality of wheat, e.g. where it grows, when it was sown and harvested, the type and condition of the soil, climate, etc., but the main differences are between soft and hard wheats.

Soft wheat has a lower protein content, and thus less gluten than hard wheat; it is usually winter-sown and grown in moist, temperate conditions. The flour it gives is good for making cakes and biscuits. British-grown wheat is normally of this variety.

Hard-grained wheat contains more protein, and thus more gluten, which makes it excellent for bread and pasta. It is spring-sown, and harvested in warm dry conditions. American and Canadian wheats are often of this type. In practice, hard and soft wheats are frequently blended to provide flour for specific purposes. The protein, vitamins and minerals in wheat are distributed throughout the grain, but as you can see from the drawing of a wheat grain (opposite), a substantial proportion of the nutrients are contained in the outer edges. It is this portion of the grain that is removed when the grain is milled to produce white flour. The more of this outer layer is removed, the lower the extraction rate of a flour. Generally, as the extraction rate decreases, the quantities of nearly all the nutrients fall off rapidly. If you enjoy white bread but still want to benefit from the goodness of wheat, you can buy bran and wheat germ – which are removed during the production of white flour, and which contain much of the goodness – and add them to your diet in other ways.

Brown and White Bread

To get the best nutritional value out of wheat, we should buy or make bread from 100 per cent wholemeal flour milled on stone rollers. This does not take the question of taste or appetite into account however, and on occasions we may prefer a lighter, blander-tasting but less nutritious bread than the wholemeal variety. Who, for instance, can resist a freshly baked French loaf?

The nutritional qualities of different breads are illustrated in Table 5 which shows the nutrient contents of flours of various extraction rates. White bread is made from flour of 65 per cent to 70 per cent extraction, and brown breads from flours of 80 per cent to 100 per cent extraction.

Table 5 *Nutritional Content of Flours of Different Extraction Rates*

Type of flour	Protein	Fibre	Carbo-hydrate	B₁	B₂	Niacin	Iron	Calcium
	(gm per 100 gm flour)			(mg per 100 gm flour)				
100% (wholemeal flour)	12·2	2·00	64·1	0·37	0·12	5·70	3·50	36·0
81% (brown bread)	11·7	0·21	70·2	0·24	0·06	1·60	1·65	—
70%	11·3	0·10	72·0	0·08	0·05	0·80	1·25	—

Rice

Rice and wheat are the world's most important foodstuffs. Nearly a half of the world's population depends on rice as their staple food, and a fair proportion of this number rely almost solely on rice for their nutritional needs. Most rice is grown and consumed in Asia, particularly the Far East, and a substantial amount of this rice is consumed by the farmers and families that grow it. Much of the remainder of the world's rice crop is produced in the USA, Brazil, Spain and Italy.

In Britain most of the rice is imported from America, and more recently there has been a certain amount from Australia, which, unexpectedly, became a rice source as a result, indirectly, of the Second World War. The Australians had their rice supplies cut off by the Japanese and were prompted to start cultivating their own.

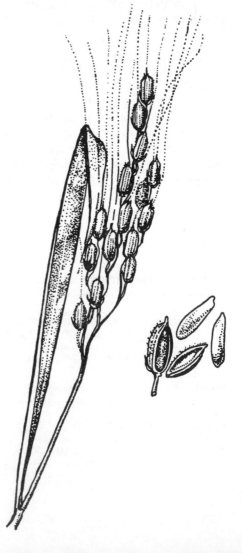

Rice is an excellent crop for populous areas short of space. It gives a better yield and requires less seed per acre than other cereal grains, and under the right conditions two crops a year may be cultivated. Further, natural, unpolished rice (brown rice) is of good nutritive value with an excellent balance of vitamins, minerals, protein, fat and carbohydrate. Finally, and perhaps most important of all, rice is easy to cook, satisfying to eat and easy to digest.

A predominant characteristic of rice-eating peoples is their great preference for rice over other foods, and given extra spending power they normally prefer to buy more rice than add other grains to their diets. In a small way I understand this desire for rice; I spent a year in Japan, and during this time ate rice with every meal. On my return to England I was surprised to discover I was longing for rice, even for breakfast!

The botanical name for rice (*Oryza*) is derived from the Latin *oryzon*, which some scholars suggest derives from the even earlier Tamil word, *arisi*, meaning 'rice without husks'. Another theory is that the name was given by the Chinese Emperor Chin-nung. He ruled in about 2800 BC and was responsible for the first clear written record of rice. Rice did not, however, originate in China but in India. By piecing together tiny fragments of evidence, historians believe that domesticated rice was developed from the seeds of a wild Indian grain called '*Newaree*'. From India, rice spread eastwards to China and Japan and westwards to Persia and the Middle East. The Persians introduced it to the Greeks, and the Greek poet, Sophocles (495–406 BC) mentioned it as a 'God bestowed' food. During the medieval wars between Moslems and Christians, the Moors occupied Spain and took rice with them. It became very popular, and by the sixteenth century had spread to Italy (although some suggest Marco Polo introduced it there in the thirteenth century) and from there to the south of France.

Rice never grew wild in the Americas (so-called 'wild rice' indigenous to that continent is not the same species), although in 1647 an Englishman, Sir William Buckly, tried to cultivate it in Virginia. He was unsuccessful in his efforts, and it was to be another fifty years before rice was finally introduced to Americans. The captain of a ship bound for Liverpool from Madagascar found the ship had been blown off course, so decided to put into Charleston, Carolina for repairs. Colonists who visited the ship included a man with the fine name, Landgrave Thomas Smith; he discovered that the ship was carrying unhulled rice and asked for a small bag to use as seeds. He planted them in some local swampy fields, and they grew well. Four years later Carolina exported its first shipment of rice to England. Although most rice now grown in the USA is from states other than Carolina, the French still call long grain rice *riz Caroline*.

The rice plant

Many varieties of rice have been developed to suit the different climates, soils and methods of cultivation of particular areas, and rice is grown within a surprising range of latitudes that includes the northern and southern limits of the temperate zone; optimum yields, however, are obtained in the humid tropical and subtropical zones of the world. These many varieties have their origins in two species. The most important is *Oryza satiya*, a white grain rice originally cultivated in the monsoon belt of South Asia, and the other is *Oryza glaberrima*, a red grain rice first grown in Central Africa.

Rice plants grow to between 2 and 5 feet tall depending on the variety. They have a central stalk to which long, smooth, narrow leaves are attached. While rice is growing in the fields and before husking, it is known as 'paddy rice'.

Rice plants can be broadly divided into indica or long grain rices, and japonica or short grain rices. Strangely, although japonica plants give higher yields per acre than indica, there is normally a definite preference for indica in areas of the world where rice is a staple crop. These long grain rices remain in separate grains when cooked, and become light and fluffy. Japonica rices, popular in Japan and parts of China, are soft cooking and the cooked grains tend to stick to one another.

Rice is the only major cereal crop that is planted in water. (There are dry land rice varieties, but they are not as common as the aquatic.) The plant likes abundant supplies of fresh water, and it is estimated that it requires 300 gallons of water to grow 1 pound of rice! It grows with its roots constantly submerged but with the leaves above the surface of the water taking in oxygen and transporting it to the roots. Unfortunately, this peculiar characteristic of rice requires that its cultivation, unless mechanized, involves many hours of back-breaking work.

In the first stage of rice growing, a seed bed is planted. The seedlings are allowed to grow a few inches and then the bed is flooded. The rice plants are grown to nearly a foot before the bed is drained, and they are then carefully transplanted by hand, one by one, to a flooded paddy field. The plants are given time to establish themselves before the field is drained for weeding and hoeing. Finally the field is flooded again and the rice ripens ready for harvest. In modern rice-growing countries, all these operations are mechanized and the rice is even sown by air straight into the fields. In primitive areas, nature controls the process and the farmers have to wait for the monsoon rains to flood their fields. Many of these farmers grow a fascinating variety called 'floating rice', which can grow very fast – up to a foot a day – and so keep its head above the flood waters.

Humanity seems to thrive on adversity and, despite all the hard work involved in cultivating rice, the flowering paddy fields have inspired Eastern poets through the centuries. The Chinese poet Sun Tung-Po, writing in the eleventh century about his own efforts at growing rice, begins one of his poems as follows:

> I planted rice before Spring Festival
> And already I'm counting joys,
> Rainy skies darken the Spring pond;
> I chat with my friends by green-bladed paddies.
> Transplanting takes till the first of Summer,
> Delight growing with wind-blown stalks.
> The moon looks down on dew-wet leaves
> Strung one by one with hanging pearls.

Rice and Nutrition

After the rice paddy has been harvested, it is dried and threshed and the unhulled rice grains are separated from the rice stalks. This rough rice is then hulled by gentle crushing and the thick woody husk surrounding the grain is removed by winnowing or other methods, leaving the whole rice grain. As with wheat, this wholegrain (or brown) rice contains all the nutrients naturally present in the grain. Again, as with wheat, it has become normal to mill off the outer layers of the grain to give white rice. In doing this, many of the vitamins, the minerals and much of the protein are lost, since they are collected in the outer shells or bran of the rice grain. The difference in nutritional content between brown and white rice is illustrated in Table 6. As you will see, rice can be an excellent source of B complex vitamins, vitamin E, calcium and phosphorus.

Table 6 *Nutritional Content of Brown and White Rice*

Components	Brown rice	White rice
Protein (%)	8·9	7·6
Fat (%)	2·0	0·3
Carbohydrate (%)	77·2	79·4
Fibre	1·0	0·2
Vitamins (parts per million)		
Vitamin C	0	0
Thiamine (B_1)	3–5	0·6–1·0
Riboflavine (B_2)	8–1·0	0·28
Niacin (B_5)	55	15–20
Minerals (% × 1000)		
Calcium	84	9
Phosphorus	290	96
Iron	2	0·9
Potassium	342	79

There are of course some dishes that are best prepared with white rice (e.g. sushi rice), but I prefer brown rice. To me it looks more wholesome and appetizing and tastes better than white rice and I cannot really understand why it is not more popular. It's clear that my view is not shared by everyone; Fran Lebowitz in her funny book, *Metropolitan Life* (Arrow, 1980), describes brown rice as 'ponderous, overly chewy, and possessed of unpleasant religious overtones'!

The rice grain and types of rice

Brown rice

Rice minus its hull or husk with the germ pericarp and aleurone layers intact. Contains all nutrients naturally present in the grain.

Converted or parboiled rice

Rice prepared from unhulled rice that has been soaked in water, steamed and dried before hulling and milling. Contains most of the original nutrients.

White rice

Rice with its outer layers of pericarp, aleurone, and germ removed by milling, causing considerable loss of natural nutrients. These are sometimes replaced artificially to give enriched white rice.

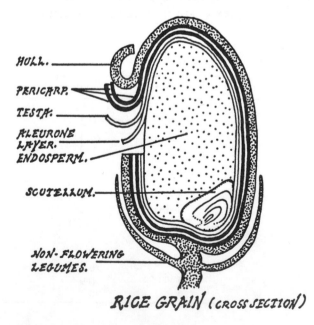

RICE GRAIN (CROSS SECTION)

Rice bran

This consists of the aleurone, testa, pericarp and germ (removed to leave white rice). An excellent source of B vitamins, minerals and protein. Add it to sweet dishes, breads, biscuits (cookies), pancakes, etc.

Rice polishings

The inner bran layers and part of the endosperm removed when white rice is polished. Milled fine and sold as flour, used to make noodles, to thicken soups, etc.

Rice flakes

White rice flaked in a power mill. Prepared for its quick cooking properties. Used in soups and puddings. Brown flakes now available.

Rice flour

White rice ground into flour and used in puddings, sauces, confectionery, pasta and bread (mixed with wheat flour).

Long grain rice

Often called 'patna rice', since it was thought to have originated from Patna in India. The grain is from 4 to 5 times long as wide, and if milled it is milky white in appearance. When cooked, the grains separate and become light and fluffy. Excellent for serving on its own as well as in pilaffs, risottos and other savoury dishes.

Medium grain rice

The type of rice first grown in Carolina, America. It's shorter than patna rice, but the grains are a little more plump. Basmatti rice from India is of medium length but much thinner even than patna rice.

Short grain (or round grain rice)

A short plump grain rice, most popular in Japan and parts of China. It's sticky when cooked and in the West is usually reserved for making puddings. It is, however, well suited to being eaten with chopsticks, which may account for its popularity in Japan, where it is always served plain and unsalted as an accompaniment to a savoury dish.

Italian rice

Another short grain variety and, as its name implies, cultivated mainly in Italy. The grain absorbs more water than other types of rice, and is used for making dishes such as risottos in which the sauce is cooked in with the rice.

Wild rice

A cereal grain native to North America, China and Japan. It belongs to the same broad family as the rice plant, but is not an ancestor in that the rice we cultivate today did not develop from this particular wild grass. It is a very beautiful plant growing in areas of abundant fresh water. The Red Indians would collect the grass by floating alongside the ripe plants and then gently pulling them over the boat while they knocked the delicately held grains into the hull. The plant is difficult to grow domestically, and is consequently expensive. Nutritionally it's very rich and contains more protein and vitamins than regular rice. Raw wild rice is brown, but it acquires a faint purplish colour when cooked. It has a delicate nutty flavour.

Corn

Corn grain is not nutritionally as complete as whole rice or whole wheat. However, whole corn kernels or whole corn meal is more nutritious than either white rice or white flour, and eaten in combination with other foods, particularly beans, it is an excellent food source. Corn is more generally eaten in its whole form than either rice or wheat and this, coupled with its adaptability to different growing conditions and its ease of cultivation, makes maize a valuable food crop worldwide. America, where corn is their most valuable annual food crop, is the world's largest producer, but substantial amounts of corn are grown in many other countries.

Wild corn has never been found, nor has any wild predecessor been identified. In the Americas, corn has been a staple domestic crop for thousands of years, and the indigenous Indians developed a diversity of types. It now flourishes from northern Canada to Argentina. In Europe corn was unknown until the end of the fifteenth century when Columbus brought some of the grain back from his discovery voyage to America.

The botanical origins of corn will possibly never be discovered, but the Indians of Ecuador tell a story abouts its beginnings which is much more colourful than the real one is likely to be.

Many thousands of years ago there was a terrible flood and only two Indian brothers survived. They did so by climbing to the top of the highest mountain in the land. Just as they were about to die of hunger and thirst, two gaily coloured parrots flew to them with food and drink, both made from the maize plant. The brothers were revitalized

and one of them quickly captured one of the parrots. It turned into a beautiful woman who gave them maize seeds and taught them how to plant and grow the crop. She became the mother of the first Indian tribe and maize became their basic food.

Maize and nutrition

Before discussing the nutritional qualities of maize or corn, we should note the difference between dent corn, which is grown for use as a cereal grain, sweet corn or corn on the cob which is grown for use as a vegetable, and popcorn. Sweetcorn is too soft and too sweet to be dried and ground into a flour. Its protein content is slightly higher than many other vegetables, but lower than that of dent corn; its nutritional worth should really be compared with that of other fresh vegetables rather than other grains. Popcorn is made from a variety of corn with particularly hard endosperms. If the corn is heated rapidly the endosperms burst with a loud bang, hence the name. Popcorn is poor nutritionally and should really only be considered as a fun food.

Whole dent corn or maize has the highest nutritional value. It contains substantial amounts of phosphorus and iron and thiamine (vitamin B_1) and smaller quantities of riboflavin (B) and carotene, the precursor to vitamin A. Wholecorn has an average of 9 per cent by weight of protein. Eaten with other foods, particularly beans and vegetables, whole maize or corn is an excellent addition to the diet.

The maize grain and types of maize

The bran, which comprises 5 per cent to 6 per cent by weight of the grain, is contained in the protective, tough, fibrous outer layer of the grain. Maize flour or meal, in which the bran is sifted out, is called bolted corn flour. Some valuable roughage and minerals are lost in the process.

The endosperm forms the main part (80 per cent to 85 per cent) of the grain and contains much of the protein and most of the starch. It can be divided into three sections. The first is a one-cell deep outer layer or aleurone layer, which is rich in protein and fat. The second section underneath the aleurone layer is the horny or tough part of the endosperm. This region is much harder than the corresponding areas of the rice or wheat grain and gives corn meal its characteristic grainy texture. The third inner section is called the flour endosperm, and is a softer, mainly starchy region.

The germ of the grain contains the nutrients needed for the development of the grain or seed into a plant. It is much larger than its

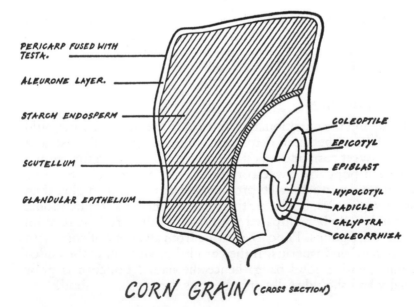

CORN GRAIN (CROSS SECTION)

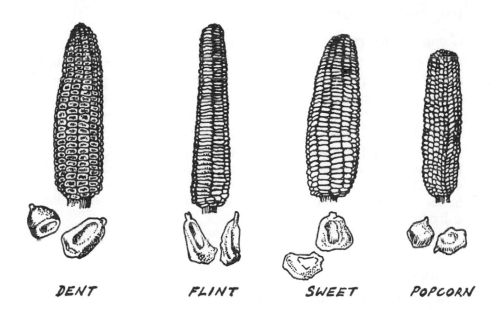

DENT   FLINT   SWEET   POPCORN

equivalent in rice or wheat and is rich in fat and protein. Half of the fat is composed of linolin which gives linoleic acid, one of the essential unsaturated fatty acids needed but not synthesized by the body.

The following definitions refer to dent corn products, dent corn being the variety from which nearly all commercially available cornmeals or flours are made. The broad top of the grain has a longitudinal groove or dent from which its name derives.

Whole maize

To prepare whole maize the grains are dried on the cob and then removed. However, maize is rarely eaten in this form since milling it into flour increases its digestibility, and the variety of ways it may be used. Tinned or frozen whole corn kernels are obtained from sweet corn on the cob, not dent corn.

Whole maize or cornmeal

The whole grain is ground into flour of 95 per cent to 100 per cent extraction. This meal retains all the goodness of the corn. Stoneground is best if you can obtain it.

Bolted maize or cornmeal

The whole grain is milled and then the coarse bran pieces are sifted out. This is 90 per cent to 95 per cent extraction meal or flour and it contains most of the goodness of the grain. It is better than whole maize for preparing breads or other dishes where a smooth mixture is desired.

Cornflour (degerminated maize meal)

Made from the whole grain with the bran and germ parts removed. Gives a flour of 85 per cent or less extraction. Not as nutritious as whole maize flour, but excellent for thickening soups, sauces, etc.

Hominy flour or grits

Hominy, an old American food sometimes called 'samp', is made by treating kernels of corn with an alkaline solution, which dissolves the skin. They are then washed several times in water, boiled for some hours and finally dried. Hominy grits are made by coarsely milling dried hominy.

Oats

Until the early nineteenth century, oats were the main cereal crop of much of Scotland and northern England, and widely used for bread-making. They were, however, considered very much a working class food and Doctor Samuel Johnson wrote, 'oats are a grain that is

generally given to horses, but which in Scotland support people'. The reply of a wise Scotsman was, 'and that is why in England you have such fine horses and in Scotland we have such fine men'. Oats are a tasty food and a rich source of protein, vitamins and minerals.

The name 'oats' derives from the Old English word *ate*, which is from the Old English verb *etan*, to eat. Samples of the common cultivated oat (*Avena satira*) have been found in cave dwellers' sites in Switzerland dated from 1000 to 2000 BC. Although there is no real evidence of where or when it was first cultivated, the crop thrives in cool, temperate climates and it possibly originated in northwest Europe where two wild grasses, wild red oat and common wild oat, are found. These wild grasses are particularly successful at broadcasting their seeds and for thousands of years oats were considered not a food source but a weed amongst other cereal crops. Hence the phrase 'sowing wild oats', or, as the Oxford Dictionary defines the phrase, 'indulging in youthful follies'!

Whole oat grain is generally equal to or richer in protein than either whole wheat or rice. The grain is rarely hulled and it is a good source of B vitamins, particularly inositol, as well as the minerals iron and phosphorus. Other trace minerals and vitamins are also present. Eaten with dairy produce oats provide a well-balanced diet.

Oatmeal

Oatgrains or groats as they are sometimes called, are usually sold as oatmeal or oatmeal flour. There are three types of oatmeal available. The first type, a large flat oatmeal, is prepared by rolling the husked oats but not cutting them. They take quite a long time to cook. The second variety is prepared by cutting the oatmeal into flakes before rolling it. This medium sized oatmeal cooks more quickly than the first variety. Instant or quick cooking oatmeal is made by this process but the oats are heated before rolling. It is possible that some nutritional value is lost during heating. Steel cut, later known as Scotch oatmeal, is the third variety. The steel-cutting process was pioneered by an American called Ferdinand Schumacher in the nineteenth century. He made his fortune from the process and later became known as the 'Oatmeal King'. His method simply consisted of cutting the oat grain into several pieces on steel blades. Some nutritionists consider steel cut oatmeal to be the best form of oats.

Oats are also ground into flour available in coarse, medium and fine grades. The grade chosen for a recipe is usually just a matter of taste.

Oatmeal is used principally in breakfast foods (e.g. porridge, muesli, mush, etc.) and to a lesser extent in savoury dishes, soups and stews. Oatmeal flour is used in making breads, cakes and scones.

Barley

Barley was the chief food crop of the ancient Roman and Greek civilizations. The Roman goddess Ceres is usually represented with ears of barley plaited into her hair or crown, and the same symbol appears on ancient Greek and Roman coins. The Roman naturalist Pliny believed barley to be man's oldest food crop and certainly evidence has been found of its use in Egypt as far back as 5000 BC. Barley is one of the hardiest of all the food grains, it has a wide growing range and rich nutritional value, comparable with the other major cereals.

The name 'barley' derives from the Old English word *baerlic*, with the same root as *beow*, meaning 'to grow'. An even older name is *bere* and the connections between barley and brewing are remembered in our word for that famous drink, beer!

The many varieties of barley are subdivided according to the number of rows of grain there are along the ear of the plant. The most common type in ancient times was six-rowed barley, and this variety is still an important food crop in parts of India, Tibet (where it is the only crop that will grow – the altitudes being so high) and in Japan where barley is second to rice as a staple grain. Other popular varieties are the four-rowed common barley and the two-rowed coffee barley.

Barley contains very little gluten and consequently cannot be used to make light, risen breads. Instead it is used to make flat breads and cakes, porridge, soups and stews.

Barley has also been used in brewing for thousands of years; it was from the yeast obtained as a by-product of malted barley that the first yeast wheat breads were made.

The widespread cultivation of wheat and rice led to a gradual worldwide decline in the importance of barley and by the sixteenth century in Europe, barley was important only in isolated areas (e.g. in the Isle of Man, barley was a staple food crop until the nineteenth century). Nowadays barley is principally cultivated for use in the brewery industry and for animal food, although it is well suited to human consumption.

Wholegrain barley contains an average 11 per cent by weight of protein, valuable vitamin B and important minerals.

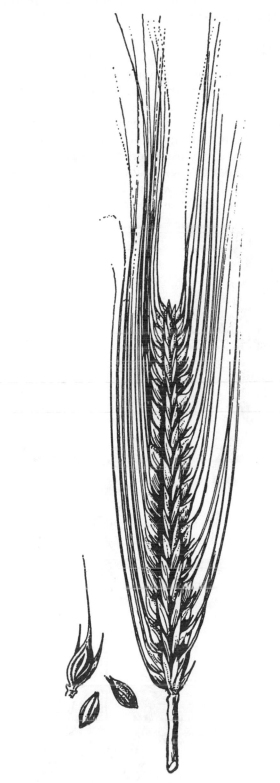

TWO ROW

FOUR ROW

SIX ROW

Millet and sorghum

Millet is said to have been the first cereal grain cultivated by man. Plants of the millet family, including sorghum, are prolific growers and they can be grown very successfully even with primitive farming methods. 12,000 years ago, before the introduction of rice, millet was the staple food in China. Today it is still a major food crop in parts of Africa, Asia and India. It is a particularly useful crop in areas likely to suffer drought, since during long periods without rain the plant stops growing but thrives again once there is water. Millet has a short growing cycle and under suitable conditions 2 crops a year can be sown and harvested.

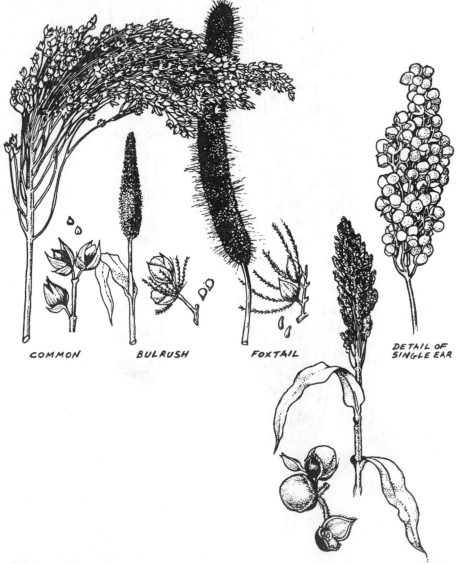

COMMON   BULRUSH   FOXTAIL   DETAIL OF
SINGLE EAR

In the West, millet is generally demoted to animal food, but why this is so is a mystery. Nutritionally millet compares well with other cereals, and the cooked grains and flours are delicious. It contains vitamins of the B complex, important minerals, especially iron, and 9 per cent by weight of protein. Millet grain is always hulled since the outer part is too hard to cook. Fortunately this does not involve a large nutrient loss, and millet grain is almost as nutritious as whole millet flour which includes the milled hull or bran section of the grain. Many peoples with long life-expectancy, including the famous Hunzas of the Himalayas, cultivate millet as a staple crop.

The general name 'millet' derives from the Old English word *mil*, which itself was derived from the Latin name *milium*. Common millet, the most widely grown member of the millet family, is known by a host of other names including French, Indian, white, hog, broom (the branches of this plant are well suited for making brooms) millet and the old Slavic name, *Prosso*. There are two other popularly grown millets: pearl, cat-tail or bulrush millet, and fox-tail, Italian or yellow millet. This latter plant is the most widely used millet for human consumption in Britain and the USA. It is easily identified from other millets by its light yellow, small, spherical kernels.

Sorghum, a member of the millet family, is little known in the West but it is a cereal grain of major importance in many parts of Africa, and was ranked only behind wheat, rice and corn in world food consumption in a recent United Nations survey. Sorghum originated in Africa many thousands of years ago. In prehistoric times it was introduced into Egypt and from there spread to Asia, reaching India and China where it is still an important crop. The Spaniards introduced sorghum to the New World via Mexico, and nowadays sorghum is cultivated in both North and South America for animals.

There are many varieties of sorghum but the most important in terms of food for human consumption is great or dourra millet. It has large white seeds and is the leading cereal in Africa.

Nutritionally sorghum is similar to common millet although on average the protein content of sorghum is a little higher (11 per cent compared with 9 per cent by weight). Sorghum grain is usually eaten unmilled and sorghum flour is made from whole unhulled grains. Both these factors add to sorghum's nutritional worth, particularly in areas where it is a staple food crop.

Rye

Rye grass is thought to have originated in an area close to the Caspian Sea. It is closely related to wheat but in ancient times was considered to be just a troublesome weed rather than a food source. Late in the history of the Roman Empire, the Romans started to plant rye as a crop and by the Middle Ages rye was a staple grain in much of Europe. In medieval Britain, rye and barley bread was as popular as the wheat variety; rye bread is still common in Scandinavian countries, Germany and parts of Russia. Rye was introduced into the USA by early European settlers. It became popular both as a food and for making rye whisky, for which much of today's rye is grown.

Although rye itself does not share the distinguished history of wheat grain, ergot, a fungus that grows on rye grain, probably had a considerable metaphysical influence in medieval Europe. Ergot, from which the drug LSD is derived, has the same effect on the central nervous system as this very powerful hallucinogen and under damp conditions it forms a mould on growing rye grains. Flour made from these grains and eaten will have bizarre effects on the consumer, and historians believe that many of the 'devil-induced' plagues of the Middle Ages were probably caused by such a phenomenon. I wonder how many witches died at the stake for eating rye bread?

Rye flour contains less gluten than wheat flour and consequently rises less in the bread-making process. Rye bread is flatter and more filling than yeasted white bread. It has a distinctive taste and texture. Thin slices of dark rye bread are excellent for preparing Danish-style open sandwiches. Breads made with both wheat and rye flours combine some of the qualities of both grains and are also popular.

Dark rye flour is prepared from the whole grain while the lighter coloured rye flour has had some of the bran removed. Whole rye grains or groats may be used in the same way as wholewheat grains or brown rice while cracked rye (grits or flakes) cook more quickly and are useful in stews, soups and cake-making.

Whole rye grains or flour are an excellent source of the B Vitamins, particularly niacin. They contain an average 12 per cent by weight of protein – which compares well with rice, wheat and corn – and a significant amount of important minerals.

Buckwheat

Although buckwheat is commonly regarded as a grain, it is in fact the seed of a herbaceous plant called brank buckwheat which is native to Central Asia. It was brought to Europe from Russia by the Tartars and was first cultivated in Germany in the fifteenth century. It was from the German *buchweizen* or beechwheat that the name was derived since the seeds of the plant resemble the seeds of the beechnut tree. In Italy buckwheat is called *faggina* while the name of the beech tree is *faggio*. Saracen wheat is another name for the seed; this refers to the belief that the Crusaders introduced the plant into Europe.

Buckwheat grows to a height of about 2 feet, it has heart-shaped leaves and beautiful pink flowers and is sometimes grown as a garden flower. In areas of Russia where the plant grows wild, buckwheat honey is a great favourite. It is a tough, hardy plant that will grow in the harshest conditions without requiring much attention. The seed is expensive, however, since the outer husk is difficult to remove and the grower must either invest in expensive equipment or time-consuming methods to process his crop.

The hulled grain is normally roasted before use and this roasted seed, or 'kasha' as it is called, is popular in parts of northern Europe as well as being part of the national cuisine of Russia. Kasha has an interesting nutty flavour and it makes a pleasant change from the regular grains. It is served both as a side dish, in the way that potatoes or rice may be, and as an ingredient in savoury dishes. The crushed seeds, called 'groats' cook more quickly than kasha. They are used in the same way as ordinary kasha or in sweet dishes and breakfast cereals to add crunchiness to the texture. Roasted groats are readily ground into flour if you have a hand grinder at home.

Buckwheat flour is used to make pancakes, muffins, cakes, etc. The flour is rather heavy and expensive and is usually mixed with lighter, cheaper flours such as wheat.

Buckwheat contains valuable amounts of all the B vitamins as well as quantities of minerals, particularly iron and, on average, 11 per cent by weight of protein.

Pulses

Beans, peas and lentils are the seeds of plants which belong to the family of plants called pulses. Pulses, together with cereal grains, were the earliest food crops cultivated by man. They grow in a wide range of climates and provide an excellent protein and carbohydrate source as well as some vital vitamins and minerals. Eaten in combination with cereal grains, pulses can provide all the essential amino acids needed by the body.

The Leguminosae or bean family is a huge one. It contains over 14,000 species and it is the second largest family of seed plants. These leguminous (meaning pod-bearing) plants have the valuable property of fixing atmospheric nitrogen in nodules in the roots of the plant and converting it into nitrates which enrich the soil in which the plant grows. They are thus of double value as both food source and fertilizer and are particularly important in areas of the world where fertilizer is not available or is too expensive for farmers to buy. The edible seeds of the leguminous plants are the parts we eat. The dried seeds – what are generally meant when discussing pulses or legumes – are seeds left on the plant to ripen in the sun and become fully mature. Fully ripe seeds have a tough outer skin which is why they store so well and also why they need soaking before being cooked. Of the enormous Leguminosae family only about twenty species are cultivated in appreciable quantities.

The English word 'pulse' is derived from the Latin *puls* or *pultis* meaning 'pottage' or 'porridge'. It was first used by the French and was introduced into the English language after the Norman invasion in the eleventh century. It became the most commonly used word to describe beans and peas although scholars writing in the seventeenth and eighteenth century preferred the term 'legumes'. 'Pulse' never gained popular usage in America.

The cultivation of legumes has a long history in human civilization and an ancestory as distinguished as that of the cereal grains. Remains of field beans and lentils, radiocarbon dated to 6000 or 7000 BC, have been found at neolithic sites in the Near East. Remains of beans more than 5000 years old have been discovered at sites in Mexico. These finds even pre-date the earliest remains of domesticated maize. Lentils were well liked by the Ancient Egyptians and extensively cultivated. Apart from providing food, lentils also served an unusual role as a packing material when the infamous Roman Emperor Caligula shipped an obelisk from Egypt to Rome. The obelisk is still standing to this day (perhaps with a few very old lentils tucked away in secret cracks). The Egyptians, however, were not fond of other beans (particularly broad beans, for some reason) and the priests forbade their use believing that each one contained the soul of a dead man! Pythagorus, who introduced many Egyptian ideas into his religious theories, believed the same. Legend has it that he was killed by the soldiers of Dionysus; they had ransacked Pythagorus's home town and were in hot pursuit of him and his followers when suddenly he stopped and gave up rather than cross a bean field. Other Greeks felt differently towards beans and Plato, a vegetarian, regarded them as a vital requirement for a long and healthy life. The Greeks even had a God of Beans called Kyanites to whom they dedicated a temple. The Romans had mixed views. Funerals were followed by a 'bean feast' but generally beans were thought to be fit only for peasants. Broad beans were used as counters in voting matters. White ones signified a vote for, and black ones a vote against, and during election times candidates for office generally distributed white beans among their followers.

Nutritional value

Beans, peas or lentils in their dried forms contain as many calories per weight as grains and in general twice as much protein. The protein content of most pulses varies between 15 per cent to 25 per cent and is as high as 38 per cent for soya beans. Further, legumes, if properly soaked and cooked, are well digested by the human body. Although the amino acids (which are essentially proteins) of legumes are rich in lysine they are low in sulphur-containing amino acids and this means all the proteins present are not available to the body. However, cereal grains are lacking in lysine and rich in sulphur-containing aminos – just the reverse of legumes – and if the two are eaten in combination they provide a full complement of all the essential amino acids. Soya beans are the exception since they contain, on their own, an exceedingly high proportion of good quality protein.

Legumes in general contain little fat, 1 to 2 per cent for the majority of beans, rising to 4 per cent for chickpeas. The figure is much higher for soya beans (18 per cent) and peanuts (also called ground nuts), both of which are used as sources of vegetable oil. Although low in content, the fats present in legumes are usually rich in essential fatty acids. They are also a good source of the B vitamins thiamine and niacin, and the minerals calcium and iron. Cooked, dried legumes do not contain vitamin C, but sprouted beans are an excellent source (see page 107 for methods of sprouting beans).

General instructions for the preparation and cooking of pulses is given in Part Two.

Individual pulses: beans, peas and lentils

Aduki bean

The aduki plant is small and bushy and there are many varieties. The seed of the bean is small, shiny and red and it is most popular in the far eastern countries of Japan, Korea and China. It has a sweet taste and apart from its use in savoury dishes, the cooked, mashed beans are used as a sweet filling in cakes and buns. In Japan, the aduki bean is thought to have curative properties particularly for kidney complaints. These beliefs have recently been supported by medical evidence. The aduki bean is also rich in protein and is known as 'the King of Beans' by the Japanese.

Black beans

Alternative names for this bean are turtle soup beans and *frijoles negros*; a smaller variety are called Chinese black beans. It is a member of the *Phaseolus vulgaris* group of beans.

A black shiny bean popular in South America and the Caribbean, it is slightly sweet and particularly good in soups and casseroles. In the Caribbean it is traditionally flavoured with cumin, garlic and a spicy tomato sauce. The smaller variety popular in China is normally fermented with salt and served in small quantities with fish or chicken. Black bean sauce is also a popular Chinese accompaniment to main dishes (it is sometimes made from soya beans).

Black-eyed beans

Also known as cowpea and blackeye pea, this bean's botanical name is *Vigna unguiculata*.

It is white or creamy with a black or dark yellow eye. The yard-long bean or asparagus bean, which grows pods 3 feet long, and the field pea are members of the same family. The black-eyed bean plant is a native to Africa but it is now also cultivated in India and China. Spanish explorers took it to the West Indies in the sixteenth century, from where it spread to the Americas.

Black-eyed beans were fed to the slaves carried from Africa to America; they are now traditionally served with rice in black communities in the USA on New Year's Eve to ensure a lucky year ahead. In Africa the young pea pods are eaten as a vegetable and the leafy shoots eaten like spinach. Black-eyed beans, pork and sweet potato are said to be a splendid combination.

Broad beans

Alternative names are fava, wox, Windsor and Horne, while the botanical name is *Vicia faba*.

Both creamy-white and brown varieties are available. Broad beans have been grown since ancient times and remains have been found on the Bronze Age sites of lake-side dwellings in Switzerland. They were very popular in Britain in the Middle Ages and important enough to warrant the death sentence for their theft from open fields. They were mainly dried and saved for use in the winter months, hence the proverb, 'Hunger makes hard beans sweet'.

Immature pods can be eaten as vegetables, as can the young green beans. The mature dried beans need a good soaking and long cooking before use. They are popular in casseroles, salads, puréed or in pies.

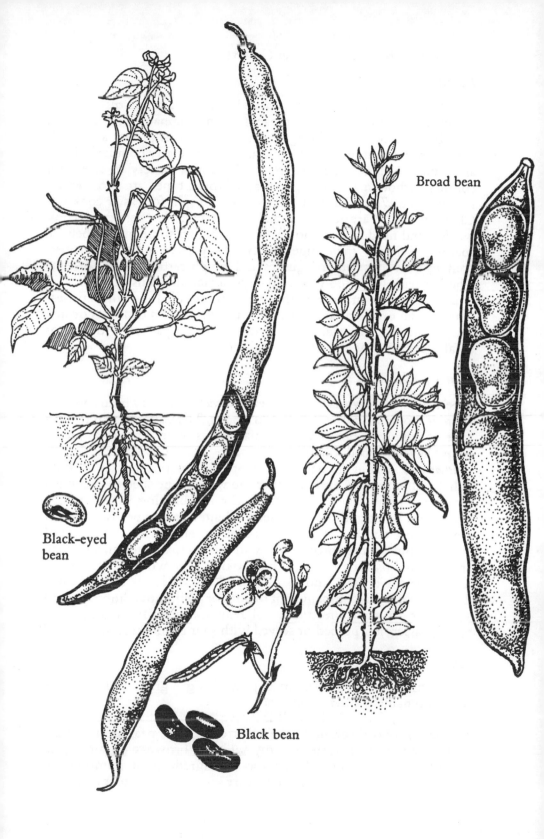

Black-eyed bean

Black bean

Broad bean

Lentils

Also known as red dhal or split pea, its botanical name is *Lens esculenta*.

One of man's oldest foods, the lentil plant originated in South East Asia but was cultivated in Egypt and Greece. It is grown as a cold-season crop throughout the tropics and is particularly popular in India and South America. Lentils are available in a variety of sizes and colours, although the red, green and brown types are most easily found in the West. Red lentils are often sold split for easier cooking. Chinese varieties are generally smaller than Indian lentils. Lentils cook quickly and need little or no soaking, although some people believe soaking increases their digestibility. They have a higher protein content than most other legumes and a high carbohydrate content. They provide good food for cold days or labour-intensive work.

Lentils are used in India for the preparation of dhal and other curries. They are an excellent accompaniment to vegetables or meats or in a soup. One word of warning – lentils are often packed with lots of small stones or grit and need careful picking over.

Butter beans

Alternatively known as the lima bean, sieva bean, curry bean and pole bean, its botanical name is *Phaseolus lunatus*. The butter bean is really a type of lima bean but since the lima bean is better known as butter bean I have included it here.

Phaseolus lunatus is native to tropical America but it is now cultivated in tropical areas all over the world. The species is divided into two groups, the small-seeded, dwarf, climbing variety which gives sieva beans and the large-seeded butter-bean types with which we are more familiar. The large-seeded varieties grow in a range of colours from white to brown. They all contain toxic substances which are removed by long soaking and cooking. The white variety is less toxic than the brown, and is sold, dried or canned, as butter beans. They are a good accompaniment to pork or poultry or combined with sweetcorn to make the traditional American dish succotash, or in soups, casseroles, puréed or served with sour cream in salads.

Chickpeas

Otherwise known as Garbanzo peas, Bengal grain and ceci, the botanical name is *Cicer arientinum*.

This is my favourite bean. It is native to the Mediterranean region but now grows throughout the sub-tropics. The peas are normally yellow but are sometimes creamy white or brown with a dimpled surface. They are most famous as an ingredient of hummus (or houmous) in which the cooked peas are ground to a paste mixed with

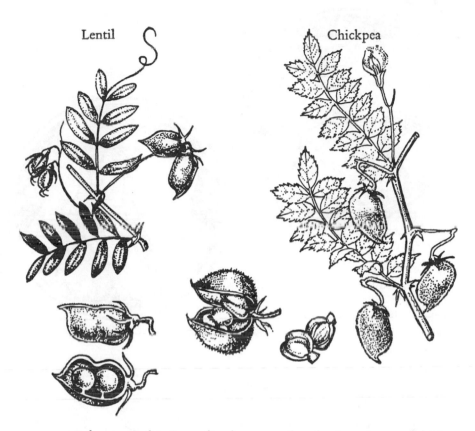

Lentil

Chickpea

sesame-seed paste (tahini), garlic, lemon, oil and salt and served with pitta bread. They are also an ingredient of falafel; ground chickpeas are flavoured with onion, parsley, cumin and coriander in this recipe then rolled into walnut-size balls and deep fried.

The peas are most nutritious and their cultivation as a protein supplement is being encouraged in India.

Kidney beans

The bean's botanical name is *Phaseolus vulgaris*.

This species of bean is the most commonly cultivated in the world today and includes all the various types of haricot beans. It is from this group that the famous and ubiquitous baked beans in tomato sauce are prepared. The kidney bean is native to America and has been grown by the indigenous Indians since prehistoric times. Columbus brought a number of varieties to Europe and they quickly became popular and widely cultivated. The French took a liking to them and they are sometimes still known as French beans. The following all belong to the kidney bean family:

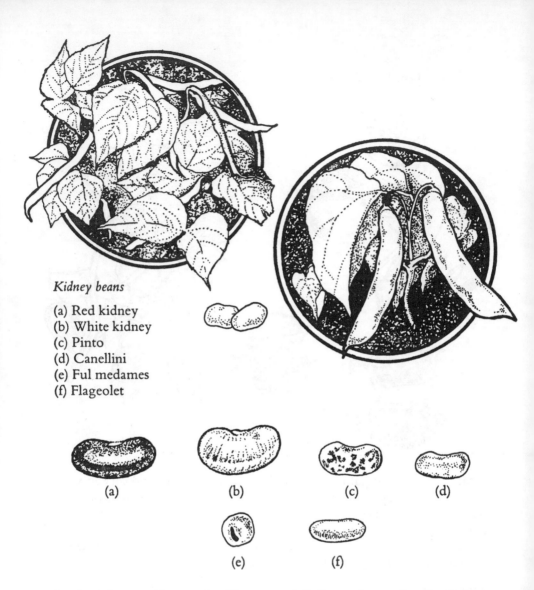

Kidney beans

(a) Red kidney
(b) White kidney
(c) Pinto
(d) Canellini
(e) Ful medames
(f) Flageolet

(a)　　　(b)　　　(c)　　　(d)

(e)　　　(f)

Barlotti beans: Grown in Kenya and Italy and popular in Italian cookery, they are available in both brown and white. They are the main ingredient in Venetian bean soup, in which barlottis are cooked with ham bones and spices, served with noodles and topped with Parmesan cheese.

Canellini: Small white haricot beans from Argentina, these have a slightly nutty flavour.

Egyptian kidney beans (ful medames): These are similar to the hyacinth bean, field bean and Dutch brown bean. Native to India but popular in Egypt and the Near East, they are very tasty but need long soaking and cooking. In Egypt they are a national dish and they even have *ful*

(Egyptian for 'bean') cafés. Traditionally they are boiled with cumin, seasoned with garlic, lemon, and oil, and served with chopped parsley and boiled egg.

Fagioli: This is an Italian white haricot bean.

Flageolets: These delicate, pale green, young haricot beans have a subtle taste. Grown in France and Italy, they are usually only available in tins outside these countries.

Haricot beans: This smallish, tender white bean, is the main ingredient in many traditional dishes. It is similar to the American navy bean, the Great Northern bean and other beans called white beans.

Pearl bean: A small haricot bean.

Pink beans: Grown in Mexico, these are often eaten refried (see Pinto bean).

Mung beans

Also called the green gram or golden gram, the mung bean's botanical name is *Phaseolus aureus*.

A small olive-green bean, rounded with flattened curves, it originated in tropical Asia and is still most widely grown in India and South East Asia. Mung beans contain an exceptionally high vitamin A content for a legume, as well as vitamin B and a little vitamin C. The mung plant grows quickly and several crops can be harvested every year. For this reason it is excellent for growing bean sprouts and in China the beans are used solely for sprouting. The bean sprouts most commonly available in both Britain and the USA are grown from mung beans. It is closely related to the black gram or urd bean which is grown throughout the East, both for sprouting and for milling into flour.

Pigeon peas

Its alternative names are gunga and yellow dhal, and its botanical name is *Cajanus cajan*.

A perennial vine, this yields for 2 to 3 years and gives small, round, flat peas speckled with brown marks. The plant originated in South East Asia but is now most popular in India where its drought-resisting properties are useful. It is also popular in the Caribbean where, together with rice, it forms part of the staple diet. The young seeds can be eaten fresh as a vegetable or dried and used like lentils.

Pigeon pea

Pea

Peas

Also known as the common pea and garden pea, the pea's botanical name is *Pisum sativum*. Many varieties of this annual vine are available, ranging from dwarf to tall, and smooth skinned to wrinkled. The plant originated in the area between the Euphrates and the Tigris rivers known as the Garden of Eden. It is now grown in temperate regions throughout the world.

The pea plant has a long and illustrious history; remains have been found in the ruins of ancient Greece and Egypt. The word 'pea' is derived from the Sanskrit *pis* meaning 'piece' or 'piece of pod'. In Latin this became *pisum* and finally in early English *pease* (whence pease pudding). Throughout Europe in the Middle Ages peas were grown and dried for use as a winter food. They were generally preferred to both beans and lentils. Strangely, it wasn't until the seventeenth century that fresh peas in the pod became popular. Suddenly, at the court of Louis XIV, young peas or *petit pois* became all the fashion and nowadays, of course, frozen or tinned peas are much more common than the dried variety, although split peas are still popular.

There are two main types of common pea. The first and most popular for human consumption is the garden pea; the second is the field pea, considered inferior in taste to the garden pea and grown as animal food. Commercially available garden peas have been separated into shape and size and are sold according to their sweetness and starch content. Thus we have sugar peas, snow peas, petits pois and marrowfat peas ranging from the sweet to the starchy.

Yellow split peas: These are used in soups and casseroles and, in India, like lentils for preparing dhal and rissoles.

Green split peas: Famous in pea and ham soup, green split peas are also a major constituent of the northern English dish pease pudding. They are good in soups, stews and casseroles and as an accompaniment to fish and chips.

Peanuts

Also known as ground nuts and monkey-nuts, the botanical name is *Arachides hypogaea*.

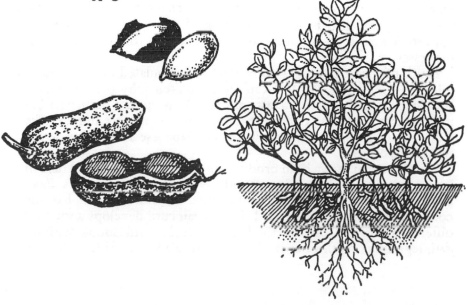

The peanut is strictly speaking a legume and not a nut. It is best known to us in its salted and roasted form as a snack food although grown principally as a source of vegetable oil. The plant originated in the tropical forests of South America. It was taken back to Europe and Africa by Portugese and Spanish explorers and reached North America via slave ships which carried peanuts as food.

Peanuts contain a high proportion of essential fatty acids and peanut butter should be a nutritious food. Unfortunately, to increase the shelf life of their product, manufacturers hydrogenate the butter and thus turn its essential oils into fats good only for providing calories. It's worthwhile making your own peanut butter, a simple process (see page 109), or being sure to buy it from a reputable wholefood store.

Soya beans

Alternatively known as soybean or soya, its botanical name is *Glycine max*.

Soya beans are the most nutritious of all the legumes. They contain as much high-quality protein as steak and further contain unsaturated fats that can actually reduce cholesterol levels in the blood. The soya bean is the first legume of which written records are available and its nutritional importance has been recognized for thousands of years. Emperor Shen Nung of China in 2800 BC included soya beans in his description of the five principal and sacred crops of China (the others being rice, wheat, barley and millet). His advisers published exact accounts of how the crop should be cultivated and the plant spread quickly to Japan and other areas of South East Asia.

In the last twenty years there has been a huge boom in the use of soya beans in the West. This largely followed the financial measures taken by the US government to encourage farmers to grow more of the crop, parallelled by the application of advanced technology to convert it into food products and raw material for manufacturing processes.

Much of the extra crop is converted into simulated meat products which, to me, taste awful; I can see no reason why manufacturers should try to make this food taste or look like meat. It is quite possible to make excellent natural foods that have their own tastes and textures from soya beans, and the Chinese and Japanese have done it for thousands of years.

The three main soya bean products they make are bean curd (*tofu* in Japan), bean paste (*miso* in Japan) and soy sauce (*shoya* in Japan). Bean curd is a fermented soya bean product. It is white and has the consistency of a delicate custard. Fried bean curd develops a tougher outer coating and can be used in casseroles and soups without disintegrating. Fresh bean curd is used in salads, as a side dish or in

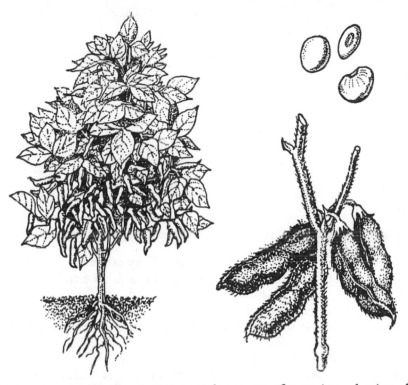

ways we may use cheese. It is a rich source of protein and minerals, contains no fat and is an aid to digestion.

Miso is a fermented soya bean paste that keeps indefinitely; its flavour even improves with age. Combined with rice or other grains, miso supplies all the essential amino acids and also contains enzymes that are helpful to the digestion process. It is a versatile ingredient and is used as a base for soups, salad dressings and sauces, as a marinade for fish, meat or vegetables or as a spread.

Soy sauce is the best-known soya bean product. Its appearance on the tables of Chinese restaurants has probably misled many people about the true taste of soy sauce. The stuff on the tables is normally an artificially flavoured, chemically based liquid that has only a passing association with real soya beans. Real soy sauce is made from a mixture of soya beans, wheat and salt, fermented together for up to two years, then mashed and filtered. It is available but is more expensive than the chemical stuff. 'Tamari' is a brand name for real soy sauce.

In the East, soya beans are not usually soaked and boiled whole like other legumes, but then there is no great tradition for casserole-type dishes there. In fact whole dried soya beans lend themselves best to this style of cooking. Long soaking and cooking times are essential if the true flavour of the beans is to be appreciated and if the dish is to be completely digestible.

Nuts

Nutritional value

Nuts are fruits of certain trees and bushes. They normally consist of a hard or tough outer shell which encloses the edible kernel – the nut. Although they are best known as a snack food, nuts are a delicious, highly concentrated food with a wide range of cooking possibilities. They are a valuable source of proteins, vitamins, minerals, fats and fibre.

The snack-food type of nuts we are most familiar with are prepared by roasting the raw nuts after coating them in a saturated fat. They are then heavily salted. In this form, nuts are not a particularly healthy food, nor are they easily digestible. In the following pages we refer only to natural untreated nuts. They are best bought loose, not prepacked, from a shop that sells nuts in bulk. It pays to shop around since prices seem to vary considerably. Also, broken nuts, which are perfectly good for most cooking purposes, are often much cheaper than the whole variety.

Below are descriptions of each of the common nuts listed in alphabetical order. Instructions for preparing nuts for cooking are given in Part Two.

Individual nuts

Almonds

Almonds are possibly the most popular nuts. They have been cultivated since very early times and they are mentioned in the Old Testament. The small trees appear to have originated in the Middle East and their fruit has been an important commercial product in Syria and Egypt since biblical times. They were later cultivated in Greece, and the Romans called almonds 'Greek nuts'. The tree spread westwards across Europe and from there to the temperate regions of America, Australia and South Africa.

In the spring the tree produces a beautiful pink and white blossom, followed by the formation of a green fruit which contains the seed or nut. The tree is closely related to the peach tree. The nut is coated with thin, dark brown skin, which can be eaten or peeled off after light blanching in boiled water.

Two types of almonds are grown – one bitter, one sweet – and it is the latter variety we are most familiar with. Bitter almonds are broader but shorter than their sweet cousins and they contain a small amount of prussic acid, which is responsible for the bitter taste. The acid, although poisonous, is volatile and can easily be removed by heating. Bitter almonds are most often used for the production of almond oil, although occasionally they are required in dishes with a bitter flavour. Sweet almonds are used extensively in Middle Eastern and Indian cooking. They can be cooked whole or used ground in puddings, cakes and pastries. Marzipan is a mixture of almond paste and sugar.

Almonds contain protein of higher biological value than any of the other common nuts. They are also a good source of B vitamins and unsaturated fats. Uncooked almonds are an excellent addition to salads, fruit dishes and breakfast cereals and a small amount of ground almonds will give an unusual flavour to regular soups and sauces.

Brazil nuts

Brazil-nut trees are native to the tropical region of Brazil where the nuts are collected on a commercial scale. They are also found in the forests of Venezuela and Bolivia but not in commercially viable numbers. The trees, which grow very straight and tall, have never been successfully cultivated and the nuts are always collected in the wild. The familiar three-sided Brazil nuts grow on the tree inside a large, woody, coconut-shaped pod, within which they are packed like segments in a grapefruit. A falling pod, which can be the size of a

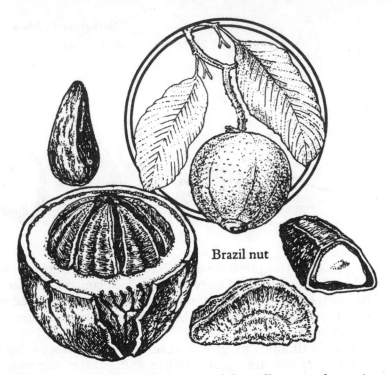

Brazil nut

human head, could easily kill a man and the collectors who go into the Amazonian forests to gather the nuts need to wear protective helmets. Once found, the fallen pods are cracked open on the spot with a machete and the nuts, still in their individual shells, are extracted. From the forests the nuts are transported up the Amazon to the town of Para, a great marketing centre for Brazil nuts, and thence they are exported around the world. Surprisingly the Brazilians themselves do not consume many of these nuts and nearly the whole crop is exported.

Brazil nuts have been popular since Victorian times as a dessert nut, eaten either raw or salted, with a glass of port after dinner. In more recent years they have become popular in the manufacture of chocolates and chocolate bars. There are, however, a number of other culinary ways in which they may be used and they are also a rich source of protein, unsaturated fats and vitamin B.

Cashew nuts

Cashew nuts actually grow on the outside of a pear-shaped fruit. This fruit is, however, not a real fruit and it merely serves to divert interest away from the cashew nut which is the real fruit of the plant. To add to the confusion, the mock fruit is known as a cashew apple and in areas where the tree grows the apple is normally more popular than the nut. The plant succeeds admirably in its plan to draw attention away from the nut!

The trees are native to Brazil and the name cashew is derived from the Brazilian Indian word *acaju*, which the Portugese explorers mispronounced as *caju*. Portugese colonizers introduced the trees into Goa in India, from where the plant spread to other parts of the country. India now exports much of the world's supply of cashew nuts, growing its own crop as well as processing those of other countries.

The nut is enclosed in a shell which contains an acid fluid harmful to the skin and the nuts are always sold both shelled and slightly roasted to ensure all vestiges of the fluid are removed before consumption. Cashew nuts have a well-balanced combination of proteins, fats and carbohydrates and they are a particularly nutritious food.

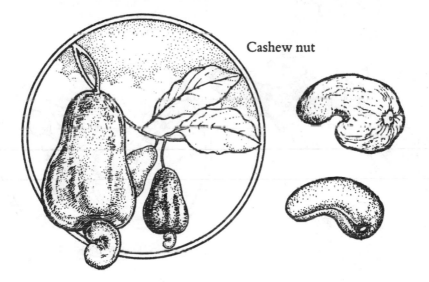

Cashew nut

Hazelnuts, cobnuts and filberts

Hazelnuts, cobnuts and filberts are closely related nuts wich grow on small trees or shrubs belonging to the Corylus family of plants. Originally they were native to the temperate regions of northern Europe and Asia but they are adaptable plants and these nuts are now cultivated in many parts of the world. The wild species were collected by the Romans and were an important food source for the marching armies. In Britain, hazelnuts are still the most common of wild nuts.

The nuts occur in clusters of twos and threes and each is partly covered with a green helmet-shaped skin. Hence the name 'hazel' which derives from the Anglo Saxon word *haesil* for 'headdress'. In ancient Greek times, the best hazelnuts came from Avella in the Campagna district of Italy and the specific botanical name for the tree

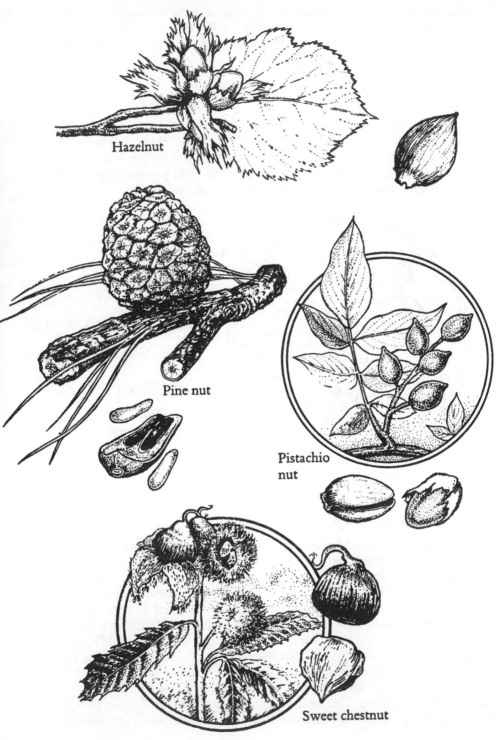

Hazelnut

Pine nut

Pistachio
nut

Sweet chestnut

is *Corylus Avellana*. The name filbert is probably derived from St Philbert, whose saint's day on 22 August coincides with the ripening time of the nut.

The nuts may be eaten fresh, roasted, ground or chopped, and they are widely used in the manufacture of chocolates and other sweets. They have wide application in the kitchen and may be used in salads and main dishes as well as desserts. They are a good source of proteins, vitamins, fats and minerals.

Pine nuts (pignolias)

Many different species of pine trees yield edible seeds which are collectively known as pine nuts or pignolias. The nuts grow inside the hard outer casing of the familiar pine cone and they grow unshelled. They are usually white or cream in colour with a soft texture and a flavour of turpentine if unroasted. The pine nuts most commonly available in Europe come from the stone pine, a tree native to Italy which is now cultivated all around the Mediterranean coast.

Many different types of pine trees with edible seeds are grown in North America but this food source has never been exploited except by native Indians who collected the nuts for winter food.

Pine nuts, if cooked with other foods, impart a delicious and distinctive flavour and they are popular in Middle Eastern and Italian cooking. I find them particularly delicious when sprinkled on top of a gratin dish just before baking or grilling.

Pistachio nuts

The pistachio nut is very popular in America where its pale green colour makes a distinctive ice-cream. It has a venerable history and pistachios have been grown in the warmer parts of Asia for thousands of years. They are now cultivated in the Mediterranean countries of Europe, the Middle East, India and on a large scale in the south-western states of America.

The nut grows in a thin shell which conveniently cracks open at one end when the nut is ripe. In Europe and America pistachios are normally eaten as dessert nuts or used for decorating sweets and pastries. In Middle Eastern countries they are used as important ingredients in savoury dishes. They are a good source of vitamin A as well as protein, unsaturated fats and minerals.

Sweet chestnuts

The chestnut tree is native to the Mediterranean area but it was carried to northern Europe by the Romans and is now widespread through Europe. It was given the name sweet chestnut to prevent confusion with the horse-chestnut tree, a different species only introduced into Europe in the last 300 years. The seeds of the horse-chestnut are not true nuts and have a bitter, unpleasant taste.

In southern Europe, particularly Italy, sweet chestnuts have been a staple food for thousands of years. They are eaten roasted, stewed or dried and ground into flour for bread and porridge. Chestnuts available for export, mostly produced in France, are either the regular chestnut, called *chantaignes*, or the best-quality chestnuts called *marrons*. It is from the latter that the famous *marrons glacés*, sweet glazed chestnuts, are prepared.

In Britain the climate is too cold for the chestnut to ripen properly and the British have traditionally imported sweet chestnuts from Spain, hence the old term, 'Spanish chestnuts'. In America, native sweet chestnuts have been almost wiped out by a parasite and their future in that country lies with the botanists who are trying to develop a hybrid tree resistant to the disease. The Chinese and Japanese also cultivate chestnuts, and dried Chinese chestnuts bought at a Chinese store are generally cheaper than their European equivalent.

Chestnuts are not such concentrated foods as other nuts and they contain less protein and fat and more carbohydrates. They are, however, easily digestible and an excellent energy source. Serve them roasted or boiled with vegetables or salad as you may do rice or potatoes. Chestnut flour may be used in cake-making and the purée is good in stuffings, sauces and desserts.

Walnuts

Walnut trees are native to Iran but, as with many other plants, they were carried into many parts of Europe by the Romans and they are now widespread. The nut and its shell are the 'stone' inside the green, plum-size fruit of the walnut tree. The fruit appears in mid-summer, later turns brown and splits open, dropping its stone, the walnut, onto the ground.

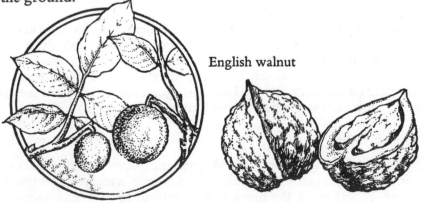

English walnut

The black walnut, which is different in shape and flavour and has a harder shell than the ordinary variety, is native to America. In America the European walnut is known as the English walnut, whilst in Europe it's sometimes known as the Italian walnut. The latter seems more suitable since, although it was once common and could be found in parks and gardens all over the country, nowadays the walnut tree is rare in Britain. A huge demand for walnut wood at the end of the eighteenth century resulted in many trees being cut down.

Walnuts, and particularly the black walnut, are a good source of protein and unsaturated fats. They also provide valuable amounts of B vitamins and the minerals iron, phosphorus and potassium. Black walnuts are also rich in vitamin A. The nuts are excellent in pies, stuffings, breads, casseroles, salads and as a topping on gratin dishes and cakes. The unripe nut can be pickled and the raw nuts are good with cheese and fruit.

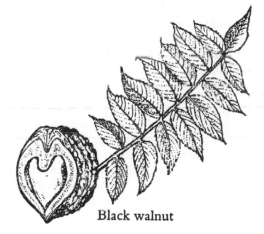

Black walnut

Glossary

Bolt	to sieve coarse grain to remove the bran
Bran	the fibrous outer layer of wheat or other cereal grains
Bulgar wheat	wholewheat grains parboiled, dried and then cracked
Burghul	another name for bulgar wheat
Congee	a thin porridge or gruel made from rice or millet
Corn	English word meaning staple grain but also used more specifically for the cereal grain called maize in America
Corn on the cob	name used in Britain for fresh sweetcorn still on the cob
Corn dodger	type of corncake
Corn flour	white or yellow corn finely ground
Couscous	large grains of semolina. Couscous is also the name of a dish prepared by steaming couscous and serving it with a meat or vegetable sauce
Dark rye	flour made from the whole rye grain
Durum flour	variety of hard wheat used in the manufacture of pasta
Endosperm	the main part in mass of a cereal grain. It is principally starch with some protein
Extraction rate	describes the proportion removed of the nutritious outer part of the wheat grain before it is milled into flour. The lower the extraction rate the more has been removed and the less nutrient the resultant flour contains
Farina	flour made from the endosperm of cereal grains. Used for puddings, soups and cereal dishes
Germ	contained within a cereal grain it is the embryo of a new plant. It is rich in nutrients
Grits	coarsely ground cereal grain. The word normally refers to hominy grits
Groats	whole or partially milled grains of hulled cereal grain. Most often used in connection with buckwheat and oats
Hard flour	flour made from hard-grained wheats. Contains more gluten than soft wheat and is better for bread and pasta making
Hominy	whole kernels of corn soaked in alkaline solution, washed, boiled and dried

Hull	outer inedible covering of seed or cereal grain
Husk	same as hull
Kasha	mush made from buckwheat or buckwheat and barley mixture. Sometimes used to describe other boiled cereal grains
Kernel	whole grain, normally meaning wheat grain and also the soft parts within a hard shell of a nut
Leavened	refers to bread or cakes with a rising agent, normally yeast but also baking powder
Legumes or pulses	group of plants containing the various edible beans and peas
Light rye	rye with some of the bran removed
Meal	hulled grain coarsely ground into a flour
Mush	boiled meal, normally meaning boiled cornmeal
Oatmeal	coarsely ground oats
Paella	Spanish dish prepared with rice, meat, poultry, fish and vegetables
Pearl barley	produced by removing the fibrous bran layer from whole grain barley
Pilaff, Pilau, Pulao	all names describing dishes prepared by cooking rice with meat or vegetables. See index
Pulses	see *Legumes*
Samp	another name for hominy
Semolina	flour of various grades made from the starchy endosperm of wheat grain
Soft flour	made from soft-grained wheats. Low in gluten content and good for making cakes and biscuits
Unleavened	refers to breads made without a rising agent
Wild rice	seeds of an aquatic grass native to North America. Unrelated to ordinary rice
Wheat berries	hulled whole kernels of wheat

Cook's Notes

English–American Food and Cooking Terms

Food

English	American
caster sugar	granulated white sugar
demerara	dark brown sugar
icing sugar	confectioners sugar
treacle	molasses
biscuit	cookie or cracker
scone	biscuit
porridge	oatmeal
currant	raisin
French bean	snap or string bean
swede	rutabaga
spring onions	scallions
courgettes	zucchini
marrow	squash
cornflour	cornstarch
aubergine	egg plant
pulses	beans
butter beans	lima beans
broad beans	fava beans
haricot beans	navy beans
wholemeal flour	wholewheat flour

Cooking

to grill	to broil
to ice	to frost
to mince	to grind
tin	can
baking tin	cake pan
baking sheet	cookie sheet
frying pan	skillet

Conversions

Oven Temperatures

°F	°C	Gas Mark
225	110	¼
250	130	½
275	140	1
300	150	2
325	170	3
350	180	4
375	190	5
400	200	6
425	220	7
450	230	8
475	240	9

Conversion of Imperial Measurements to Metric

The following table was used for the conversion of imperial measurements to metric:

Ounces or fluid ounces	Grams or millilitres (to nearest unit of 25)
1	25
2	50
3	75
4	100
5	150
6	175
7	200
8	225
9	250
10	275
11	300
12	350
13	375
14	400
15	425
16	450
17	475
18	500
19	550
20	575

English–American Measurements

English

American

fluid

1 pint = 20 fl oz

1 pint = 16 fl oz

2 pints = 1 quart = 40 fl oz

2 pints = 1 quart = 32 fl oz

1 fl oz

1½ tablespoons

dry measures

flour

1 oz   4 tablespoons (¼ cup)

2 oz   8 tablespoons (½ cup)

4 oz   1 cup

butter, sugar

1 oz   2 tablespoons

2 oz   4 tablespoons (¼ cup)

8 oz   1 cup

Bibliography

BLAND, B.F., *Crop Production: Cereals and Legumes*, Academic Press, 1971
BROTHWELL, DON, and PATRICIA, *Food in Antiquity*, Thames & Hudson, Praeger, 1969
DE SOLA, RALPH, and DOROTHY, *A Dictionary of Cooking*, Constable, 1971
DOGGETT, H., *Sorghum*, Longman, 1970
DRUMMON, J.C., and WILBRAHAM, ANNE, *The Englishman's Food: A History of Five Centuries of English Diet*, Cape, 1957
FINDLAY, W.M., *Oats*, Oliver & Boyd, 1956
GREEN, S., *Guide to English Language Publication in Food Science and Technology*, Food Trade Press, 1975
GRIST, D.H., *Rice*, Longmans, 1975
HAMMOND, W., *Rice*, Coward-McCann, 1961
JOHNSON, LOIS S., *What We Eat: The Origins and Travels of Foods Round the World*, Bailey, 1972
KINSEY, C., *Oats*, HMSO, 1959
KENT, N.L., *Technology of Cereals*, Pergamon, 1966
LEANARD, W.H., and MARTIN, J.H., *Cereal Crops*, Macmillan, 1963
LOEWENFELD, CLAIRE, *Nuts (Britains Wild Larder)*, Faber & Faber, 1957
MOORE, ALMA CHESNUT, *The Grasses*, Macmillan, 1960
MORITZ, K.A., *Grain-mills and Flour in Classical Antiquity*, Oxford University Press, 1958
MORSE, C.V., and PIPER, W.J., *The Soybean*, McGraw-Hill, 1923
NICKERSON, BETTY, *How the World Grows its Food*, Ryerson Press, Toronto, 1965
PLATT, B.S., MILLER, D.S., and PAYNE, P.R., 'Protein values of human foods', in *Recent Advances in Human Nutrition*, edited by J.F. Brock, Churchill, 1961
RAYNS, F., *Barley*, HMSO, 1959
ROBINSON, D., *Wheat*, HMSO, 1959
Rodale Press editors, *Nuts and Seeds, the Natural Snacks*, Rodale, 1978
TANNAHILL, REAY, *Food in History*, Stein & Day, 1973

United Nations Food and Agricultural Organization publications

Food Composition Tables for International Use, Washington DC Nutritional Studes No. 3, Charlotte (1949) Chatfield
Food Composition Tables – Minerals and Vitamins – for International Use, Rome Nutritional Studies No. 3

Maize and Maize Diets, Nutritional Studies No. 9, 1953
Rice and Rice Diets, Nutritional Studies No. 1, 1948
Rice: Grain of Life, World Food Problems No. 6, 1966

US Department of Agriculture publications

Composition of Foods – Raw, Processed and Prepared, Washington, 1975
Nutritive Value of American Foods in Common Units, Washington, 1975
WEATHERWAX, PAUL, *Indian Corn in Old America*, Macmillan, 1954

Index